# Restored

Cheralea A. Purcell

# Restored

a firsthand account
of God's redemptive power
in the midst of divorce

Tate Publishing & Enterprises

Published by Tate Publishing & Enterprises, LLC
127 E. Trade Center Terrace | Mustang, Oklahoma 73064 USA
1.888.361.9473 | www.tatepublishing.com

Tate Publishing is committed to excellence in the publishing industry. The company reflects the philosophy established by the founders, based on Psalm 68:11,
*"The Lord gave the word and great was the company of those who published it."*

Book design copyright © 2010 by Tate Publishing, LLC. All rights reserved.
*Cover design by Amber Gulilat*
*Interior design by Nathan Harmony*

Published in the United States of America

ISBN: 978-1-61663-016-4
1. Religion: Christian Life: Personal Growth
2. Family & Relationships: Divorce & Separation
10.02.25

# Dedication

To my Lord and Savior, Jesus Christ. You are
my life giver, provider, and sustainer.

To Mike, my best friend with the deep ocean-blue eyes
that speak volumes even when the rest of you is quiet.

# Acknowledgments

Thanks to my parents, Lauris and Sharon Meek, for their encouragement, prayers, and physical support through all the days of my life. Dad and Mom, the godly heritage that you have passed on to me is something for which I am always grateful. I know that you will walk beside me no matter what life brings. I truly love you.

Thanks to Chuck and Brenda, Matthew, Melinda and Michael Crow, Kirk and Christy Jolly, Darrel and June Weeks, Sheila Simmons, Sari Davis, and a host of other friends at Central Church of the Nazarene who stood in the gap for me when I needed all the help I could get. You were the arms of Jesus holding me tight, time and again. Words can't express my gratitude.

Thanks to Em Soulia for tackling the task of editing this book. Our e-mails and times together have made me appreciate all that you have done for Christ and our church. What an amazing lady of God you are!

Thanks to my brother, Dan Meek, and his wife, Earla, and my nieces, Sarah and Bethany. I never cease to be amazed by your lives of ministry to the Lord. I have felt the strength of your prayers coming over the miles.

Thanks to my children, Kaitlyn, Rachel, Meagan, and David. Each of you own a part of my heart, and you are the reasons I know God will continue to bless me. As I watch you grow and mature, I regularly pray that God will prove greater than all your needs. In spite of the split-family life you have, I pray that you will rise above it all and soar on the wings of eagles.

Thanks to my new family of Mom and Dad Purcell; Jim, Melodie, Courtney, Tyler, and Logan Williams; Jeff, Rosalie, Justin and Jessica Barnes; and David and Michele Purcell. I didn't think I deserved the chance to be loved and embraced again, but you have welcomed me into the Purcell clan, and I am so glad. I'm learning your traditions and enjoying our family times together. Thanks for being my cheerleaders as I wrote this book.

Thanks to my love, Mike. God used you as a lifeline to save me. Very few people could step into the role of marriage partner and stepfather of four children all in the course of two months. Your daily sacrifice for the wellbeing of me and the children leaves me in awe. Most days you understand me better than I do and yet love and adore me. You make my life complete, and as we grow old together, may God continue to bless our marriage, our children, and our home.

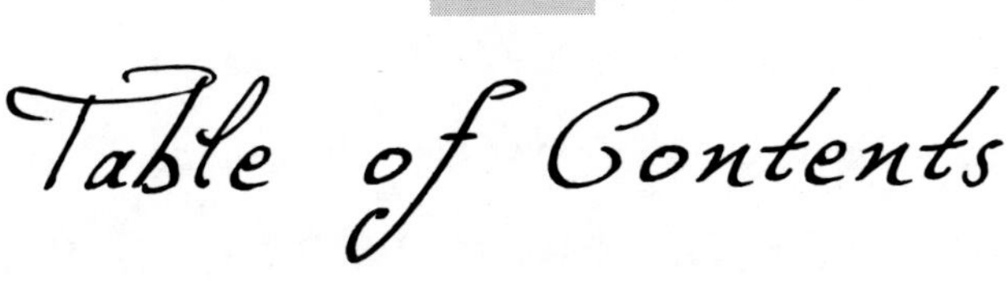

# Table of Contents

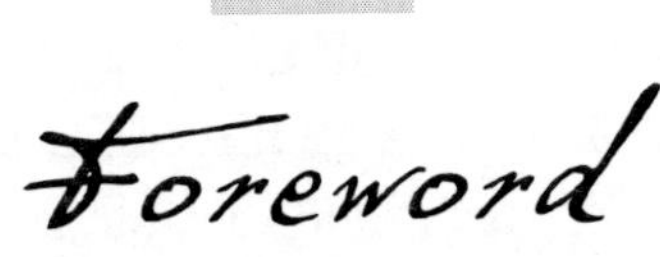

# Foreword

## By Ken Lightcap
## Pastor of Nall Avenue Church of the Nazarene, Prairie Village, Kansas

In over thirty years of pastoral ministry, it has been my experience that divorce is the most difficult road for a Christian to walk. For some it is the heartbreak of watching their own marriage dissolve; for others it is the crushing disappointment of the end of a son or daughter's marriage. For all too many, it is the tearing apart of their parents and the loss of security and certainty in their world.

The shattering experience of divorce is made all the more difficult within the church because of the reluctance of Christians to speak honestly and openly about their experiences. I suspect that often this is because the church has, in different ways, rejected those whose marriages have failed, thus compounding the rejection they have already suffered from their spouses.

However, there are courageous people who have been open and honest with themselves and with others who are lending their voices to the process of healing that these families of divorce long for. Cheralea Purcell is one of those people.

To find our way through the darkness of divorce, we need people who are coming through it themselves who will take us by the hand and carefully and wisely guide us to redemption, healing, and wholeness. Drawing on the experience of her own devastating divorce and the redemptive hope she found in the God of hope and second chapters, Cheralea offers to take the reader by the hand on this journey through the darkness together.

When divorce came to my own family, I quickly discovered that some people seemed better at comforting, encouraging, and guiding me through this new and unexplored territory. I found Cheralea to have deep insights, understanding, and a Christlike spirit that gave me hope and help for our family's journey. In this book, Cheralea is able to share with a much wider audience those same insights and encouragement through her story.

As you read this book, I hope and I pray that you will find, as did I, that you and those you love can be restored and that you will experience firsthand God's redemptive power in the midst of divorce.

# Introduction

If you've chosen to peruse this book, buy it, or consult it, you've had some experience with the depths of rejection. You are choosing to join me on a journey of discovery, healing, and redemption. This is a book based on my firsthand experience with rejection, combined with interviews, statistics, research, and a great deal of prayer. You see, God has anointed and equipped me with the gift of writing. He has also allowed me to go through the fire of rejection and divorce, and he expects me to turn that life experience into a testimony of his great faithfulness. So perhaps as you read my story, you will find yourself drawn to the Savior because despite the fact that you have been rejected, you can be redeemed and restored. The Lord is waiting to grant you new life.

# Never Say Never

## It Can Happen to You

I grew up in Middle America, where the trends from the coasts usually hit a decade later than the rest of the world seemed to experience them. I was a PK. Yep, I was a preacher's kid. I was in a safe home, comfy neighborhood, a close-knit community in a very small town. Everyone in our county seemed to know just about everyone else's business. And for these reasons, affairs were rare, or at least very well hidden. Most people married for life. Families grew old together, right along with their large farmhouses. Just as old paint peeled from the sides of the barns, so the signs of aging appeared with most couples.

They grew gray, watched their children have children, and lived out their lives together as one strong family unit.

Not until high school did I experience divorce, however distantly, when a friend's parents divorced. I never understood the root problems or heard of the reasons for the divorce, but I thought it was a horrible choice. In my experience up to that time, no one divorced. It just was not the *right* thing to do. I reasoned that all problems could be resolved with ample amounts of compromise. Oh, how immature my thinking was back then!

I remember some years later (probably in college) having a nice argument with my brother (also a pastor) about divorcees and church leadership. Back then I reasoned, *How can any pastor who has not kept his marriage vows possibly be responsible enough to lead a flock of people?* Again, what little I knew on the subject certainly kept me in the dark! I have thought of these assumptions and misinterpretations many times in the recent years, as people have treated me with everything from empathy to disdain, as if I were an innocent lost lamb or nothing better than a single mom who was determined to live off welfare. Therefore, I have learned that it is imperative that our opinions be bathed in the Word of God. What *we* think really does not matter unless it directly lines up with the inerrant, Holy Scripture.

In the early 1990s, I married my college sweetheart. We were the average college couple. We both graduated from college with high hopes and big dreams. We waited five years to start a family and then went on to have four wonderful children. Both of our fathers were pastors. Both of our families were Protestant, God-fearing, Bible-believing families going back several generations on both sides. With the exception of the usual in-law spats, our families got along relatively well. There were no major blowups between my husband and me or between our families. My little world consisted of my husband, my children, our extended families, our local church, and my part-time teaching job at a nearby private Christian high school where I taught English. I had the family I always wanted and the perfect job for our needs. The only downside was that my husband was discontent with almost every job he ever had, so our financial needs always seemed to loom over us. Juggling money was an ongoing process. However, since I was completely consumed with raising the kids, keeping up with the housework, and teaching, I left the money-juggling to my husband. I figured I had enough things on my plate to keep me busy. And for the most part, my husband worked from home, so he had the time to keep up with all those financial details.

Then, in late March of 2006, after fourteen years of marriage, my husband asked if we could have an earnest talk with each other when I returned home from a ladies' church activity. I remember praying all the way to and from church that night. I prayed out loud. I pled with the Lord. I suppose I knew in my heart that something was simply not right. In looking back, I can only think of a couple of very subtle clues that there was anything at all wrong, but at that time, I just did not get it. When I returned home from our church, my husband started off the conversation with the words I will undoubtedly remember forever. He said, "I am ninety-five percent sure I want to get a divorce."

*What? Did I hear him correctly? Did he really just use that word? Is he implying that he is not happy? What have I done wrong? What is wrong with him?* The list of questions bounced back and forth inside my head while my stomach began to tie up in so many knots that I thought I would throw up. At one point I was sure I was going to have a heart attack; my heart was pounding so hard I thought it would certainly burst right out of my chest cavity. As with all reactions to physical and emotional conflicts, my adrenalin started to pump and I directly moved into fight or flight mode. This was my marriage! This was my family! Of course, at that premature instant, the fight mode took over. I began to beg, plead, and cry for him to rethink his decision. I asked every question I could think to ask. I tried every angle of conversation, but to no avail. I went to bed that night in naïve ignorance of the real situation. I was consumed with guilt over what I had or had not done (which I had not figured out yet) and complete and unbridled fear. This was never going to happen to me! I could not even bring myself to say that nasty word. At that time, I entered the shock phase of the grieving process. Back then I had no idea this was the correct label for my emotions, but that is exactly what was happening to me.

In the shock phase, you might feel pain and numbness. Shock can also be described as instant paralysis upon hearing, seeing, or experiencing something that is an assault on your senses. When in shock, you might feel out of control or like you are going crazy. You may experience mood swings, panic, rage, relief, optimism, freedom, despair, anxiety, or just about any emotion. Common fears in this phase include fears for your survival (financially, emotionally, physically, etc), fears about the intensity of your feelings, fears about being unlovable or unable to love again, fears that the pain is permanent. You may feel panicked about the future. You might also fear what other people will think of you.[1] It took a few days for me to realize that I would not live long in a crisis mode. Either I would die of a heart attack or I would literally go insane. Yes, I was definitely in a state of shock.

# A Time of Reflection

## The Quest for Truth

As it turned out, my husband had previously scheduled a trip out of town for the better part of the following week. We agreed that while he was gone, we would both write lists of those things we were unhappy with in regard to our marriage. I am including my list from that time because I think there is merit in seeing some of the things that can be warning signs or things that can contribute to a stressful marriage. However, please do not assume that if your marriage is suffering from one or more of these details, divorce is imminent. On the other hand, it is important to see the trends that many of these things imply. We'll focus more on those trends momentarily. Here is my list of reflections:

1. My husband took no interest in our home (yard, upkeep, home improvements) other than doing what he knew he must, like periodically mowing. He didn't help with cooking, laundry, cleaning, etc. He was obviously tired of parenting young kids. He seemed to have lost personal interest in the individual lives of the children. He did no caretaking of the kids if I was in the house or yard (e.g., getting snacks or drinks, dressing, bathing, helping with the bedtime routine). He had no knowledge of or concern for the responsibilities I was juggling. He acted as though he was married to Superwoman.

2. He clearly lacked spiritual fervor. He was not "in love" with or "on fire" for Jesus. He was not the spiritual leader of our home. He lacked substantial involvement or responsibility at our church. He blamed others for his own lack of male friendships. This also meant that he had no other Christian men to help hold him accountable for his actions, thoughts, etc.

3. He tended to bank on an idea of "if then" when it came to our finances. Instead of getting and holding a steady, paying job, he lived in a financial dream world. It went something like this: "If I can start this new business in three months or less, I should be making over one hun-

dred thousand dollars within two years." In addition, he was not regularly paying tithe. He spent money without being accountable to anyone for the amount spent or how it was spent. He was so captivated by money—the need for it and the making of it—that it even superseded the preservation of our marriage and our family.

4. He rarely touched me physically, with the exception of putting his arm around me at church. He had not instigated intimacy with me in many months.

5. He was withdrawing and acting trapped. After being gone all day, he came home and went straight to the basement to work in his home office and only came up when it was time to eat. He stopped communicating with me about anything. He began to be gone from home more and more.

6. He acted resentful or even jealous that I was successful at my job and happy there. He was not verbally or substantially supportive of my school (this was also where our children attended).

7. He acted as though he was always right. He was not humble. Rather, he acted deserving of my attention and favor instead of treating me with love and basic respect.

8. He had no idea or did not care about the level of hurt he had already caused me and the kids or of the long road of recovery ahead. He chose not to love me and invest in our marriage.

As I made that list, I did not know that most of the things on that list are commonly found on another list: signs of cheating. And so, let us take a look at some of the common signs of cheating. You may find it enlightening to know that most cases are textbook. They usually bear the same overall characteristics. First, if your intuition tells you that something is not right, then it is worth investigating. However, investigating does not mean accusing. The telltale sign of a cheating spouse is seeing the need to ask that question in the first place.

Below is some information that can help you decipher what to look for if you think your spouse is having an affair.

1.  Withdraws from you, the children, and your home life: A cheating spouse stops confiding in you and seeking advice from you. He seems less comfortable around you and is touchy and easily moved to anger. He becomes accusatory, asking if you are being true to him, usually out of guilt. He shows a definite change in attitude toward everyone in the home. He loses interest in the activities in the home and even displays atypical, erratic behavior.

2.  Establishes avenues of communication in secret: The cheating spouse may set up a new e-mail account without telling you about it. He spends an excessive amount of time on the computer, especially after you have gone to bed. He buys a cell phone and does not let you know about it, or he sets up a separate cell phone account that is billed to his office. He may begin to delete all incoming phone calls from the caller ID and delete all incom-

ing e-mails that used to accumulate. He tells you that you can get ahold of him at a different telephone number. You may also receive calls that abruptly end when the caller hears your voice instead of your spouse's. The cheating husband may also use a low voice or whisper on the phone or hang up quickly when you enter the room.

3.  Physically removes himself from you and the family: He supposedly works a lot of overtime, but it never shows up on the pay stub. You find out by accident he took a vacation day or personal time off from work—but he told you he worked on those days. Your spouse is away from home, either nights or on trips, more than usual. He goes to the store for groceries and comes home five hours later. He may even sneak out of the house or pick fights with you to have an excuse to stomp out of the house.

4.  Makes unexplainable physical changes: He leaves the house in the morning smelling like Irish Spring and returns in the evening smelling like Safeguard. He has lipstick on his shirt or smells of an unfamiliar perfume or aftershave. The cheating husband may stop wearing his wedding ring. You might find items of intimate apparel or other small gift-type items that you did not give your spouse. He joins the gym and begins a rigorous workout program and has a sudden preoccupation with his appearance. He shows a sudden interest in a different type of music, style, fashion, etc.

5.  Raises hypothetical questions or scenarios: Questions are asked such as, "Do you think it is possible to love more than one person at a time?" or "What would it take for you to get really mad at me and divorce me?"

6.  Changes patterns of intimacy with you: He suddenly stops having sex with you. Or he suddenly wants more sex, more often. He may want to try new love techniques. He may try new ways to romance you.

7.  Puzzling financial matters arise: The amount of money deposited into your checking account drops off. Money is simply tighter than it was previously. Unexplained expenses show up in the bank account, but interesting and often believable stories usually follow.[1]

Now, if some of these items sound familiar to you and you are experiencing them in your home, you will want to investigate further, for as Ralph Waldo Emerson said, "Knowledge is the antidote to fear." Until you find the truth about the circumstances you are facing, you will face an even larger monster: your own fear. You don't want to live immobilized, so you must take action.

In my case, after teaching for a week under such stressful conditions, I finally shared with my principal and a select few friends what was happening. I wisely took a few days off from school and sequestered myself with my Bible, journal, and a stock of reading material at a nearby coffee shop to study up on what was happening to me. After all, I had said this would *never* happen to me. All I knew to do was go to the Scriptures and try to hear from God. In the midst of discovering pieces of things that had transpired over the past several months and years of my life, I was utterly confused by the sheer amount of information I was taking in. It finally got to a point that I was having a hard time discerning truth from hearsay and outright lies. I knew I wasn't hearing the truth from my husband. I also knew that Jesus was the way, the truth, and the life (John 14:6 NIV). With no other options, I began a biblical word study on the word *truth*. I got out my concordance and looked up and wrote down every verse in the Bible concerning the word truth. I had to ferret out the truth in my relationship with both my husband and my Lord. I desperately needed to know in whom I could place my trust.

I quickly learned to rely on that still small voice for my direction. I cried out for God to reveal the truth to me. He gave me wonderful verses of promise. Psalm 20:7 says, "Some trust in chariots and some in horses, but we trust in the name of the Lord our God." Psalm 37:3 says, "Trust in the Lord and do good; dwell in the land and enjoy safe pasture." Was the Lord really telling me that if I would put my trust in him during this, my life's darkest hour, that he would keep me safe? Wow! That was what I needed to hear. Proverbs 28:26 reaffirmed this: "He who trusts in himself is a fool, but he who walks in wisdom is kept safe." The Lord promised in Isaiah 30:15, "In repentance and rest is your salvation, in quietness and trust is your strength."

I then began to pray fervently that God would impart his divine wisdom into my very soul, guiding me in the paths of truth. And so, on many occasions since then, the Holy Spirit has told me things that have later proven true. Admittedly, sometimes it takes practice in hearing those words from God, trusting those words, and acting on them, but over time that still small voice gets louder and louder, more distinct, and set apart from all of the rest of the noise and voices in our lives. The voice of the Holy Spirit, our great Counselor, will never lead us astray.

My favorite passage on truth was 1 John 2:3–6:

> We know that we have come to know him if we obey his commands. The man who says, "I know him" but does not do what he commands is a liar, and the truth is not in him. But if anyone obeys his word, God's love is truly made complete in him. This is how we know we are in him. Whoever claims to live in him must walk as Jesus did.

# And the Judge Said

## God's Opinion on Divorce

At the time of my original Bible study, I did not know the full extent of the circumstances regarding my husband's desire for a divorce. All I knew was that I needed to be prepared for the future, no matter what. It was about that time that I began to think back over recent conversations. I thought so hard at times that I could do nothing else than unravel conversations and actions. I racked my brain for clues to my husband's odd behavior. Finally, it hit me. Two or three conversations were not lining up. I had discovered the beginning of a long string of lies. So one night when the children were at a friend's house, I headed to the basement. I went to my knees and sought holy counsel. I prayed for wisdom and discernment. I then decided to find out the cold, hard facts, the truth of what was really going on behind the scenes, yet right before my blinded eyes. I logged on to the computer and began searching through both computer and hard-copy files. I became a sleuth on a hunt for the truth. Over and over I prayed for wisdom, guidance, insight. My hands trembled with each new discovery. I took out highlighters. I went to work tracing monies spent from our account, looking up information on the Internet, etc. Finally, after what was just a few hours but what seemed like an eternity, I figured out the ugly truth. I was horrified! He was, in fact, involved with another woman. I held in my hands the "physical proof" of their relationship.

This poem sincerely expresses how I felt when the full implication of the situation hit me.

### Rejected

I am not pretty, but I am not ugly.
I think I'm just rather cute.
I am not thin, but I am not fat.
I think I'm just rather average.
I am not formal, but I do clean up nicely.
Long lashes like yours, I do not have,
But my eyes of dark brown have al-
ways been a favorite.
I have curves in the right plac-
es, and endowed I am.

Maybe I'll never be a size six again.
Maybe never size eight.
But does the tag size measure your mate?
Whatever happened to love for your soul?
Whatever happened to soul mates?
I know I am kind. I know I am gracious.
I know I try to put others before myself.
I know I have the gifts of teaching and singing.
I know that I am a good friend.
I know that I am a good listener.
I know that I try to please God.
I know that I am not perfect, but I try to be.
So what could I have done differ-
ently? Grow out my hair?
Lose twenty pounds? Have a tummy tuck?
In spite of it all, so many people tell
me that I am a wonderful person.
If this is so, why did you choose to go?
Why was I just not good enough?

Right about that time, however, the Lord brought back to my mind some faint recollection of a book written specifically for the spouse that was being left. I picked up a copy at the local Christian bookstore. While devouring this book, I found the tools and secrets that jumpstarted my ability to take back my tumultuous life. In his book *Love Must Be Tough*, Dr. James Dobson wisely counsels a jilted spouse to create a crisis, of sorts, in an effort to force the unfaithful spouse to make a choice. Dobson says, "As long as he is permitted to be 'torn between two lovers,' he can postpone a commitment and play one 'wife' against the other."[1]

It needs to be made clear to the unfaithful spouse that

he cannot have his cake and eat it, too. He must choose which woman, which life, he wants to commit to. So, after seeking help from a solid, Christian marriage counselor, I decided to make a copy of the packet of proof, hand it to my husband, allow him to read it, and then demand an explanation. Needless to say, some of these situations take a great deal of time. Lies are told, stories fabricated, guilt tossed around, etc. However, in the end, it was clear that my husband was guilty of adultery, and he decided to move out of our home.

So what was I to do? First, I had to grapple with *that* word—divorce. No matter what else was about to happen, I loved God. I wanted to live in his favor. I wanted to do what was right in his eyes. So what did *that* word really mean? I had to face *that* word. I had to deal with the very term: *divorce*. What were God's feelings toward divorce? All I had ever heard was that God hated divorce (Malachi 2:16). Great! I reasoned that if God hated divorce, then he certainly would not be too happy with me either if I had to go through a divorce. And so, I turned once again to the Scriptures. Here is what I found about God's feelings regarding divorce:

- The Lord does hate divorce. Malachi 2:15–16 tells us why. *"Has not the Lord made them one? In flesh and spirit they are his. And why one? Because he was seeking godly offspring.* So guard yourself in your spirit, and do not break faith with the wife of your youth. 'I hate divorce,' says the Lord God of Israel, 'and I hate a man's covering himself with violence as well as with his garment,' says the Lord Almighty. So guard yourself in your spirit and do not break faith" (emphasis mine). Matthew 19:3–6 further explains this when Jesus responded to a question by the Pharisees. "Some Pharisees came to him to test him. They asked, 'Is it lawful for a man to divorce his wife for any and every reason?' 'Haven't you read,' he replied, 'that at the beginning the Creator made them male and female, and said, 'For this reason a man will leave his father and mother and be united to his wife, and the two will become one flesh? So they are no longer two, but one. Therefore what God has joined together, let man not separate.'" In other words, when we took that solemn oath "until death do us part," God took that literally, and we should have as well.

- If a person is not a believer or has turned from believing in the Lord and chooses to leave the marriage and move forward with divorce, the believer must release him to go his own sinful way. In 1 Corinthians 7:10–15, Paul says in verses 12–15, "To the rest I say this (I, not the Lord): If any brother has a wife who is not a believer and she is willing to live with him, he must not divorce her. And if a woman has a husband who is not a believer and he is willing to live with her, she must not divorce him. For the unbelieving husband has been sanctified through his wife, and the unbelieving wife has been sanctified through her believing husband. Otherwise your children would be unclean, but as it is, they are holy. *But if the unbeliever leaves, let him do so. A believing man or woman is not bound in such circumstances; God has called us to live in peace"* (emphasis mine). Do you remember the old adage "Love enough to let go"? In this case, if you let go of the wayward spouse, he may see the error of his ways and come back to you. If he does not return, then you must love him enough to let him go his own sinful way.

- God "permits" divorce when marital unfaithfulness is involved. Matthew 19:8–9 says, "Jesus replied, 'Moses permitted you to divorce your wives because your hearts were hard. But it was not this way from the beginning. *I tell you that anyone who divorces his wife, except for marital unfaithfulness and marries another woman commits adultery'"* (emphasis mine). Matthew 5:31–21 states, "It has been said, 'Anyone who divorces his wife must give her a certificate of divorce.' *But I tell you that anyone who divorces his wife, except for marital unfaithfulness, causes her to become an adulteress, and anyone who marries the divorced woman commits adultery"* (emphasis mine).

- Even the Lord delineates between sexual sin and all other sins. First Corinthians 6:18 says, "Flee from sexual immorality. *All other sins a man commits are outside his body, but he who sins sexually sins against his own body"* (emphasis mine). Hebrews 13:4 states, "Marriage should be honored by all, and the marriage bed kept pure, for God will judge the adulterer and all the sexually immoral." And let us not forget one of the top Ten Commandments. Exodus 20:14 says, "You shall not commit adultery."

- The Lord himself acts as a witness in defense of those whose spouses have broken their marriage covenant. Malachi 2:13–14 says, "Another thing you do: You flood the Lord's altar with tears. You weep and wail because he no longer pays attention to your offerings or accepts them with pleasure from your hands. You ask, 'Why?' *It is because the Lord is acting as the witness between you and the wife of your youth, because you have broken faith with her, though she is your partner, the wife of your marriage covenant*" (emphasis mine). Does it make you feel better to know that our Lord is standing in the gap for you? He is your primary witness! He offers his opinion and support in all loving kindness. And praise God, he is the final judge as well!

# But I Said

## Survival of the Lonely

Now I knew what God had to say on the issue, but what was I supposed to do? I had officially entered the second stage of grief: the confusion and survival stage. A precious relationship had died, and separated and divorced people must grieve. We can't sleep. We lose weight. It is often difficult to concentrate. An old song on the radio often brings us to tears.

Below is a chart that may help you visualize how one's emotions can run the gauntlet during these phases of grief.[1]

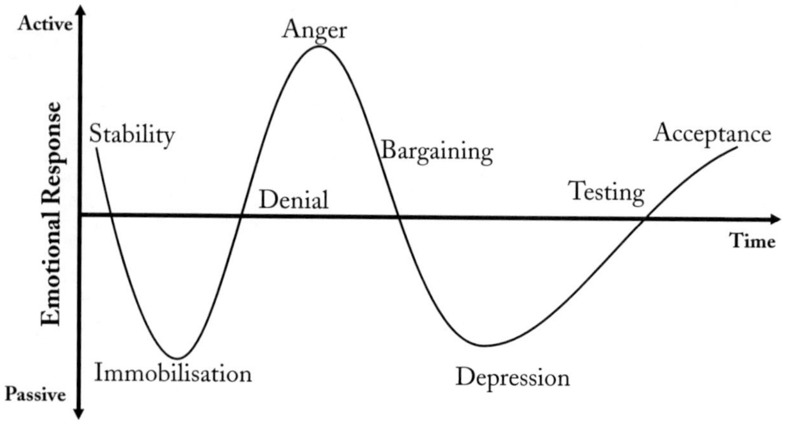


The confusion and survival stage is characterized by con-fusion and often equated with a rollercoaster ride of ups and downs. Things I did were similar to those that most "lost and left" people will find themselves doing. These may include: changing the door locks, constantly talking on the phone to "fill in" family and friends (without chil-dren hearing the conversations), staying up late, getting up early, losing weight, not being able to eat, finding myself completely exhausted. During this time, my mother was so worried about me that she convinced me to try taking antidepressants and anti-anxiety pills for a short time, but I was so foggy minded while on those that I didn't feel safe driving or being solely responsible for my children. After being on those medications for a week, I decided to hide myself in the Word and prayer and praise. I found some outlets that worked for me. Along with having a wonderful circle of family and friends who physically sup-ported me with meals, money, prayers, babysitting, etc., I also found it extremely helpful to take ample time to read uplifting promises in the Word and write them down. I typed them out and cut them apart. I then placed them all over the house—on the refrigerator, my computer, the bathroom mirrors, anywhere I found myself focusing throughout the day. I also wrote out my frustrations and concerns in a journal so that I could keep a record of all of God's provisions and answers to prayer.

### Forsaken

Shawna, Andrea, Gloria, Penny,
Who knows their names?
There were so many.
To you they were women
That helped fill a void.
But to me they each stole a bit of my joy.
With each body that you embraced
With each kiss that graced each face,
You gave away something that belonged to me.
Now here I am with my gift of love.
To whom do I give it, my one true love?
You don't think it worthy.
You don't want it, I guess.
Is there a depth to that level of sadness?
Can words quantify the meaning of rejection?
Why not me?
So now I type poems to make sense of this mess.
The poems don't rhyme;
They have no rhythm or beat.
That's just like my life, so out of sync.
One thing I know that will always be true …
My Jesus loves me, in spite of what you do.

Now let's talk about you. Do you know that you are special? Do you understand that there is not one single thing you did or did not do that justifies your spouse's poor choices? Do you know that you are not to blame for your husband's cheating ways? I realize that you (just like me) probably weren't the perfect spouse. You could have done some things differently. In fact, you may be able to list several areas that you could have improved on. However, none of those things were reasons for your spouse to turn to the arms of another person. Fred Stoeker put it this way:

> Do you still have any reason to feel that his sin is a reflection on you? Absolutely not! That's good, because you have to know it's not about your attractiveness or sexiness. It's that simple ... The tendrils of sexual sin that choke our lives aren't just sexual and aren't just physical—they reach throughout our being—body, soul, and spirit. They're about addictions and old habits. They're about wounds and emotional dependence and ignorance and warped wiring. They're about sin—his sin. Your husband is at the root of it, not you.[2]

So let's come to an understanding. Your spouse was not in right relationship with God. That is the beginning of the problem. From there, his actions began spiraling and piling one on top of the other. He was caught in Satan's trap of lies and deceit. However, he was not without freewill. He chose to take each step away from the Father. He chose to turn his back on his marriage commitment and his vows to you. He chose to betray you, sin against God, and sin against you.

He was wrong—flat wrong. Unfortunately, his sins leave you broken. But you must understand that his horrible choices were about him and his problems, not you or your problems. I know it is hard, but at this crucial moment, you need to try to find your true worth and value in Jesus Christ. Run to him for shelter and that hug that you so desperately need.

But what about the need to feel the arms of your spouse again? I remember dragging out my old body pillow from those pregnancy days. I put the long pillow next to me in bed, right where my husband used to sleep. I didn't think of it as my husband. As I leaned on that pillow each night, I prayed that Jesus would just lie down with me to give me comfort. I prayed against fears of loneliness and scary sounds in the night. I prayed for solace and much-needed rest. And I cannot recall a single night in all those months that Jesus did not give me a sweet surrender to peaceful dreams and full nights of rest.

I missed my husband in the nights; I missed him during the days. I missed the smell of his clothes as I pulled them from the laundry basket and the smell of his aftershave. I missed his voice sounding through the house and the gentle shake of the floor as he walked through the room. Simply put, I missed him.

**I Miss**
Sunday is the day of the week that I like the best.
It is the day that I look forward to above all the rest.
Getting all dressed up and ready to go
Learn of Jesus and how he loves us so.
Riding closely together in our van,
Sitting next to you, my one and only man.

Always dropped off at the door, just like a fine lady,
You would soon join me for our Bible study.
Rarely a Sunday went by that I would not hear
A compliment from you whispered in my ear.
"You look pretty today. I like your dress.
Have I told you that I love you, above all the rest?"
Knowing you were watching me from down below
While I sang in the choir in front of so many we know;
Listening to the words of life for when we cross the shores,
We got to spend some precious time together, you and I,
No one in between, sometimes a tear to wipe dry.
We sang songs of love to our Lord, our voices raising the tune.
Then it was time to head back home as it was approaching noon.
Sunday is still the day of the week that I like the best.
It is the day that I look forward to above all the rest.
I get to join with others in worshiping my Savior,
But I sure do miss sharing it with you, my friend and my lover.


Even though I missed my husband so badly, and I knew I couldn't feel his arms around me. The arms of Jesus were big enough for my every need.

About this time, I moved into the next stage of grief: hope and bargaining. I still saw some hope for reconciliation with my husband, but I knew it would be a hard and long road to travel in order to heal our relationship. At this juncture, there were a few options I saw before me. First, I could stay in my home, ask my husband to move back, and in essence, allow him to continue to defile our marriage bed. This would compromise my standards of living before the Lord a holy and upright life. I wasn't sure I could live out such a "we are doing wonderful" lie in front of my children and friends. My second option was confronting my husband with the truth and forcing him to permanently move out if he wouldn't contritely confess his wrongdoing and stop it immediately. However, either way, there were still four children to factor into the mix. I was not about to let them suffer. They would have their basic needs met by me, regardless of what their father chose to do. So without further knowledge on the subject, I decided to consult an attorney.

Now, you need to understand that when I was praying for wisdom and discernment, the Lord was paving a way for me, going before me in each step of my journey through the darkness. I felt that he looked down from heaven and shined a great spotlight on my path, making it easier for me to follow him. Choosing an attorney was one of these fascinating moments for me. You see, I had never needed an attorney before. I didn't know of a single attorney I could trust, so a dear family friend who drives a delivery route near our courthouse stopped and picked up a business card from an attorney on his route and gave it to me. After a bit of further investigation, I learned that this attorney was described by local judges as "a pit bull when you need one, or he'll back off when you want him to." Now that sounded like the kind of attorney I wanted! And so I called and set up an initial meeting with this attorney.

Heading into that meeting, I had no idea what to expect. However, the Lord was in the room with the attorney and me, and he worked in my heart and mind even as the attorney spoke to me. As I came to find out, in the state where I live, filing for legal separation had exactly the same ramifications as filing for divorce, except that the marriage remained intact. For me, that was very important. I had no intention of filing for divorce. I didn't feel the Lord leading me to file for divorce, even though I had the biblical okay to do so. Remember, "Everything is permissible for me—but not everything is beneficial" (1 Corinthians 6:12). I still wanted to leave room for God to perform a miracle and mend my marriage. Also, I never wanted the children to look back and blame me for ending the marriage, knowing I had been the one to actually file for divorce.

In spite of this, I needed to pay my bills. I needed to be able to provide for the needs of the children. I was counseled that if I filed for legal separation, child support payments would immediately commence—the court of law would recognize the need for financial assistance from my husband and the state would step in and demand that support. I left that attorney's office with a head full of new knowledge and a glimmer of hope for the future. I was in the captain's seat. God was helping me take control of the situation.

My husband was completely shocked by the legal action that I took. As with many cheating spouses, he had lost respect for me. He did not realize that I had the courage and tenacity to confront the situation he threw at me and respond with big guns flaring. I told my parents that I was stepping up to play "hard ball." I stopped relying on my husband to fix the problems, and I went after a new and different solution. I was going to see that the children were properly provided for. I was no longer going to be treated like a doormat. I was going to use my God-given reasoning abilities, my research, and my attorney to work for me. And guess what? It worked! As soon as I put action to my words, my husband realized he was in over his head. He could no longer assume that I was a naïve Super Mom who wouldn't be able to play in the big leagues. He stopped calling all the shots and started answering to the court system. In my case, the system worked with me and for me, primarily because I had a wonderful attorney representing me. Unfortunately, I realize that many abandoned men and women can't afford a good attorney or have one not worth his salt. But if at all possible, research to find the best route to get the system working with you instead of against you.

In regard to my relationship with my husband, I was still offering reconciliation. However, reconciliation was not just about convincing him to choose our children and me over another woman. It was about making major changes that proved he was sincere. I decided to write my husband a letter, specifically laying out those things that he would need to do to in order to reconcile with me.

Here are a few of those stipulations:

1.  He had to disclose all of the truth about his hidden past for the lifetime of our marriage.

2.  He had to establish a permanent residence, not living out of hotels or other long-term places. (This was for the sake of our children, who were beginning visitation times with him.)

3.  He could have no further contact with the other woman he had been seeing.

4.  He had to acquire a full-time job that paid a salary, not commission, and keep it in order to sufficiently cover our bills.

5.  Finally, he had to agree to attend marriage counseling on a regular basis with a Christian counselor.

When one pastor friend of mine heard what was going on in my marriage, he told me that there was always some measure of fault to be shared in a split marriage. I bristled from head to toe over that comment because I didn't necessarily agree with his word choice of *fault*. I do agree that there is always room for improvement on the part of both spouses. Therefore, in this letter to my husband, I admitted that I was not a perfect wife. I realized that I too needed to work on areas of my life, not the least of which was my role as his wife. However, I had remained faithful to my wedding vows each and every day of my marriage. I was sending the proposal of reconciliation to find out if my husband was willing to go the extra mile to earn back my favor.

Sending a letter has specific advantages. As in this case, I have no doubt that my husband held that letter in his hands, set it down, and picked it up again over and over. I held my copy in my hands and did the same thing. I prayed over it. I prayed over his response. I prayed for clarity to see through any traps he might set for me in his response. But I want you to know I was very firm in my resolve. Every item in that letter had to be adhered to before I was going to move forward with any kind of reconciliation. At this juncture, a truly contrite person will humble himself before his spouse and admit guilt and do his very best to not only meet every one of the stipulations, but go exceedingly further than what was even asked. If your cheating spouse doesn't want to return to the relationship because he cannot make a choice between you and his mistress, he will make up excuses, skirt his way around your demands, and ultimately decide that you are simply asking too much (obviously trying to direct some guilt your way). This is exactly what happened to me. My husband was not ready to recommit to me and me alone. He wanted to have his cake and eat it too. But that just was not going to happen.

Sometimes when this reality hits, jilted men and women will turn into the classic victims. The abandoned wife will let the arrogance and strong will of her husband turn her into a casualty. She will see herself as a used rag doll, tossed aside for something better. I too experienced waves of feelings just like these. I pictured myself being tossed aside like a dirty rag. I felt that when my husband got tired of wiping up messes with me, he rolled down the window and threw me out. The only problem was that was just the beginning. As I lay on the road, each new traveler on the journey ran right over me. Life was leaving me behind as I, the victim, lay there. I reasoned that I would rather find a sandy beach and stick my proverbial head in the sand. When the storm was over, someone could come let me know and I would regain humanity. But no, that was also a victim mentality.

So as I lay there watching my husband race out of my life, I wondered where to look.

### Grief

The tears that roll from my eye to my cheek<br>
Are only a sign of what I really seek.<br>
The wild, wild thumping of my heart in my chest<br>
Cries out for someone to understand this test.<br>
*He got in his car and drove out of my life.*

Where did he go? Is he okay?
Can anything on earth make this pain go away?
On this sad day I've lost a friend.
He was closer to me than anyone has been.
*I stood watching as he pulled away.*
No earthly person can ever be
All that my husband was to me.
The emptiness that I feel inside
Makes me cringe, run, and hide.
*The taillights of his car got smaller in my view.*
Someone tell me it's all a dream
A nightmare of sorts it would seem.
But no, my reality has a name
Sin, go away, you are to blame.
*He rounded the corner and left without a trace.*
Suffocating, choking, I'm going to die!
Please, someone tell me, why!

When I looked backward, I saw fourteen years never to be reclaimed. When I looked inward, all I saw was my crushed heart. It was gaping wide open, gushing forth the deepest imaginable pain. When I looked ahead, I was simply overwhelmed by my circumstances. How on earth was I going to raise four children as a single parent? How could I provide for their needs when I couldn't even help myself right then? And yet, when I looked upward, I saw the one who gave me hope, even in the middle of this, my darkest hour.

In her book *Anchors of Hope*, Sandi Banks says,

God had been there. And God was still there. My hurt hadn't gone away. It was real. It was tangible. But I had seen the truth of my situation in the pages of God's Word and in the hope of my ever-present Father. I didn't know exactly where I was going, but I knew God was going there with me. And that was all I really needed to know.[3]

So God had allowed this storm in my life. I reasoned, then, that he must have trusted me with it. I know he promised he wouldn't give more than I could handle, so he was going to help me handle this storm. I couldn't help but recall when Jesus told his disciples to get into the boat with him. Shortly after they set sail, the storms came up so violently that the disciples feared they would all die (Mark 4:35–38). How could they doubt the Lord? After all, he had told them to get into the boat in the first place! Didn't they trust him? And why were they surprised then that after he awoke, he simply turned to the wind and the waves and rebuked them by saying, "Quiet! Be still!" Of course, the winds instantly obeyed. Then he turned to his disciples and asked, "Why are you so afraid? Do you still have no faith?" (Mark 4:39–40). And at this point in my storm, I heard the Lord ask me the very same thing: "Cheralea, why are you so afraid? Do you still have no faith?" Occasionally he chooses to calm the storm, but more often than not, he chooses to calm his child, and I could feel him beginning to calm me.

# The Cold, Hard Facts

## The Reality of Infidelity

I tried to avoid writing this chapter, as its topic is a touchy one for me to think about, much less write about. However, after much prayer, I feel that this book would not be complete without a thorough dive into the real issues behind what has happened to those of us who have faced infidelity. Let's spend some time focusing on what has happened to our marriages.

First, let's look at Ephesians 5:28–31:

In this same way, husbands ought to love their wives as their own bodies. He who loves his wife loves himself. After all, no one ever hated his own body, but he feeds and cares for it, just as Christ does the church—for we are members of his body. For this reason a man will leave his father and mother and be united to his wife, and the two will become one flesh. This is a profound mystery—but I am talking about Christ and the church. However, each one of you also must love his wife as he loves himself, and the wife must respect her husband.

On the day you and your husband got engaged, you began the process of breaking away from your parents and creating a new life with each other. Weren't those exciting days? Do you remember counting down the months and days until you would be husband and wife? I do. I still picture myself on the phone, calling my friends and relatives to tell them that I was engaged. I vividly recall shopping and planning for my wedding. I couldn't have been happier.

At that early stage in our relationship, I knew beyond a doubt that my husband wanted to be with me in every way. He wanted to spend his free time with me. It was okay that we didn't have any money; we just wanted each other. We talked about big plans for the future. We had planned to graduate from college, get good jobs, eventually have kids, and live happily ever after. Happiness was there for us. We were having the time of our lives.

Somewhere down the road, we stopped looking at each other the same way. We stopped adoring each other the same way we did back in those starry-eyed early days of the relationship. However, those things are generally true for all couples. The "honeymoon period" usually lasts for up to two years, but by the third year of marriage, both partners begin to settle back into the relationship and display more of who they really are, dropping the façades. It is at this point that the true test of the relationship begins. Statistics tell us that around the third year of marriage, most couples face the first tough time in the relationship. In fact, I remember when we made it to our third anniversary. I was pleased that we had successfully moved past that first "hurdle."

No matter how many years your marriage lasted before you were devastated by infidelity, you have to deal with what has happened to you. So let us get to the nitty-gritty of the situation. In Ephesians, the Apostle Paul tells us that husband and wife become one flesh. Obviously this has physical, emotional, and spiritual components, so let's look at each of those.

First, when you were married to your husband, you both probably said wedding vows to each other. You promised to "keep yourself only unto him" or "forsake all others" or something similar. And so by doing this, you and your husband formed the ultimate in physical bonding. Even though you might have carried a child in your womb, there is still no closer physical bonding than that between a husband and wife. When you were intimate with your husband, you shared the most intensely beautiful moments that exist between two people. That was how the Lord planned it to be.

There is no denying the significance of the book of Song of Songs in the Old Testament. In this book, conversational thoughts seem to flow from the speakers. The lover (husband) talks to and about his beloved (wife). Sometimes their friends add comments, but the bulk of the conversation is between the marriage partners. The entire book paints a picture of the beauty of intimacy. Song of Songs 2:16 says, "My lover is mine and I am his." That certainly sounds exclusive to me. They are not sharing themselves with other people. Rather, they are saving themselves only for each other.

Here is how the wife describes the physical attributes of her husband in Song of Songs 5:10–16:

> My lover is radiant and ruddy, outstanding among ten thousand. His head is purest gold; his hair is wavy and black as a raven. His eyes are like doves by the water streams, washed in milk, mounted like jewels. His cheeks are like beds of spice yielding perfume. His lips are like lilies dripping with myrrh. His arms are rods of gold set with chrysolite. His body is like polished ivory decorated with sapphires. His legs are pillars of marble set on bases of pure gold. His appearance is like Lebanon, choice as its cedars. His mouth is sweetness itself; he is altogether lovely. This is my lover, this is my friend, O daughters of Jerusalem.

So how would you have described your husband? You probably would not have used the same similes, but if you had to compare your husband's body to various objects, what would you have said? Were his biceps like firm baseballs or his eyes like the waves of the sea? Regardless of your description, you knew your husband well. He was your lover and your friend. You shared everything with him.

The following is one of the husband's physical descriptions of his wife in Song of Songs 7:1–8:

> How beautiful your sandaled feet, O prince's daughter! Your graceful legs are like jewels, the work of a craftsman's hands. Your navel is a rounded goblet that never lacks blended wine. Your waist is a mount of wheat encircled by lilies. Your breasts are like two fawns, twins of a gazelle. Your neck is like an ivory tower. Your eyes are the pools of Heshbon by the gate of Bath Rabbim. Your nose is like the tower of Lebanon looking toward Damascus. Your head crowns you like Mount Carmel. Your hair is like royal tapestry; the king is held captive by its tresses. How beautiful you are and how pleasing, O love, with your delights! Your stature is like that of the palm, and your breasts like clusters of fruit. I said, "I will climb the palm tree; I will take hold of its fruit." May your breasts be like the clusters of the vine, the fragrance of your breath like apples, and your mouth like the best wine.

The sensuality and sexuality portrayed in this book of the Bible shows us that God created men and women with different bodies to be physically enjoyed by each other in the covenant marriage relationship. So what has happened to that relationship? When your spouse cheats on you, he shares that physical intimacy with someone else. Are there words to describe that pain? If so, I have not found them. Horrible images come to mind when we think of the person with whom we were one now sharing those wonderful physical acts with someone else. It is crushing! It is defeating! It is not right.

In that one act of making love, we also create an emotional bond with our spouses. Through those times of intimacy, your spouse learns what pleases you and what turns you on. You learn how to make your spouse happy, and you discover secrets about his body. The emotional bond between two people will never be greater than between those who have been sexually intimate together.

First Corinthians 7:5 says, "Do not deprive each other except by mutual consent and for a time, so that you may devote yourselves to prayer. Then come together again so that Satan will not tempt you because of your lack of self-control." In other words, the act of intimacy joins you and your spouse physically and emotionally. When intimacy does not occur, it is far more likely that eyes and minds and hearts will wander to other people and things. In order to help protect your marriage, you and your spouse are commanded to be intimate, to make physical love together, in order to bond emotionally.

First Corinthians 7:9 goes on to say, "But if they [the unmarried and the widows] cannot control themselves, they should marry, for it is better to marry than to burn with passion." Passion is a fierce and sometimes violent emotion. If it is not kept in check, serious pain and consequences will result. Therefore, God created the healthy, private, and purposeful act of sex between a married man and woman to give physical pleasure, as well as an outlet for many emotions, not the least of which is passion.

When your spouse has been unfaithful to you, he has joined himself physically and emotionally with another person and turned his back on all of the intimate beauty the two of you shared.

Furthermore, there is a spiritual aspect of sexuality within the bounds of marriage. Yes, sex is incredibly physical, but it is far more than that. While it is the joining of two bodies, it is also the joining of two souls. Is it any wonder that God often compares the marriage relationship to that of Christ and his church? "The body is not meant for sexual immorality, but for the Lord, and the Lord for the body" (1 Corinthians 6:13). "Do you not know that your bodies are members of Christ himself? Shall I then take the members of Christ and unite them with a prostitute? Never! For it is said, 'The two will become one flesh.' But he who unites himself with the Lord is one with him in spirit. Flee from sexual immorality" (1 Corinthians 6:15–18a).

Song of Songs 7:10 says, "I belong to my lover, and his desire is for me." And that is how it should be. But when your spouse cheats on you, it leaves you belonging to him while he desires someone else. He no longer loves you as he loves his own body. He no longer gives himself up for you to make you holy through the Word, as Ephesians 5:26–28 tells us:

> Husbands, love your wives, just as Christ loved the church and gave himself up for her to make her holy, cleansing her by the washing with water through the word, and to present her to himself as

a radiant church, without stain or wrinkle or any other blemish but holy and blameless. In this same way, husbands ought to love their wives as their own bodies. He who loves his wife loves himself.

When adultery occurs, the wayward spouse has given himself over to the lustful desire of the flesh. He has turned his back on the spiritual bond between him and his wife and turned to another person, effectually breaking his spiritual connection with the Lord as well.

Many times since I discovered my husband's infidelity, I have wondered about all those years we spent together. Did they mean nothing to him? Was his mind on our family and the times we spent together? Or were his thoughts with someone else or the times he had already been with someone else? How many times had he made love to me while he was thinking about being in the arms of another woman?

The sin of adultery has wide-sweeping physical, emotional, and spiritual ramifications. It cuts so deep we fear that the wound will never be able to heal. However, that is not true. God brings many people into our lives to help us on the journey of healing and recovery. And with that realization, I slowly entered the fourth stage of grief: letting go.

# Safety Net

## The Ministry of the Body of Christ

One of the ways God calms us is by providing us with a fabulous wellspring of friends. It helps to have a close circle of family or friends because most people are unprepared for grief since tragedy often strikes suddenly and without warning. Good friends help us deal with the pain and shock of loss until acceptance is reached. I do not understand how people make it through these dark times without Jesus. Having Jesus also means having Christian brothers and sisters, which means having friends.

Remember the quote "A true friend shows up when all the others leave"? I have had friendly acquaintances show up and treat me like royalty. They have mown the lawn, cleaned our home, brought us meals, and watched the children. They have fixed the clothes dryer, repaired the computer, and moved the furniture. They have brought groceries, filled up the tank with gas, and given cash. They have called me day and night to check on me. They have left me encouraging messages on the phone, and one even gave me waterproof mascara to help weather the storm! But most importantly, they have prayed over me, prayed with me, and prayed for me.

When I think of friendship, my mind flips back to my childhood. Valory was the first friend I actually remember and would count as a friend. We still hear from each other around Christmastime through letters. Another friend I cherish is Allyson. Our friendship bloomed in fifth grade when we were playing jacks in our classroom. We thought it would be fun to hang a staple from the electrical outlet and throw the bouncy ball at it. A few seconds later—after the smoke had cleared, after the teacher had recovered from near heart failure, and the charred wall had proven sturdy— Allyson and I realized we had something special. (After all, how many kids blow up an electrical outlet in fifth grade during in-door recess?) Although many years of almost no communication have passed, our friendship has stayed true.

Furthermore, one of my college roommates and I were together for only one semester, but we still communicate occasionally. My other college roommate lives nearby, and she and her husband have proved invaluable over the past few years. In addition, some teens I met from across our church district while at summer camps joined me at college, and we still see each other now and then.

About eight years ago, I felt the Lord prompting me to ask an acquaintance at church to be my spiritual accountability partner. Oh my, what a ride that has been! A few years later, we asked another person to join us, and both are my close friends even today. Along the way, I've acquired friends through family connections such as my sister-in-law, my husband's cousins, and my own aunts and uncles. I have also made friends through involvement as a teacher on staff at a high school (both with other teachers and my students) and as an active member in my local church. I count my Sunday school class, fellow choir members, children's workers, and staff of my church as my friends.

So I guess I have come to realize that some friends come and some friends go. Some friends are for life; some are for a time. Some friends leave footprints on our hearts and we are never, ever the same. However, there are certain qualities about friends that always remain the same, even when applied to different times and circumstances of our lives.

Here are a few things I have found regarding friends that I think are absolutely true:

1. A good friend sharpens your character, draws your soul into the light, and challenges your heart to love in the greatest ways.

2. A friend is a person who knows all about you and still loves you.

3. The greatest healing therapy is friendship and love.

4.  Friendship is God's special way of loving us through someone else.

First Corinthians 15:33 says, "Bad company corrupts good character." So who is in your circle of friends? Do they bring out your best qualities? Do you spend time with them and then go home and reflect on how much you enjoyed yourself? Do your friends say and do things that are edifying to you and to others? Or do your friends have some serious issues that leave you feeling uneasy, put-down, or confused? Proverbs 16:28 tells us that a gossip separates close friends. Are you in the company of someone with a gossiping tongue? Instead, let's choose friends who spiritually challenge us to grow in our faith, to be honest with ourselves and with others, and who say and do things that are uplifting.

A true friend is one who knows you as you really are, understands where you have been, accepts who you have become, and still gently invites you to grow. The ultimate lesson all of us have to learn is unconditional love, which includes not only loving others, but loving ourselves as well. Walter Winchell said, "A real friend is one who walks in when the rest of the world walks out."[1] And Ralph Waldo Emerson said, "It is one of the blessings of a friend that you can afford to be stupid with them."[2]

I will add that, in fact, you can even go out in public with a friend without wearing any makeup. You can wear your PJs all day, and a friend will still love you. You can be twelve years past your childbearing years and carrying those extra fifty pounds, and a friend will still love you.

You can make the worst potato salad in the entire church, and a friend will still love you. You can have past secrets and sad stories that break your very heart, but a friend will still love you. A real friend will tell you when you have spinach stuck in your teeth or toilet paper dragging from your shoe. Laurence Peter once said, "You can always tell a real friend: When you've made a fool of yourself, she doesn't feel you've done a permanent job."[3] And Dinah Mulock Craik so beautifully put it this way:

> Oh, the inexpressible comfort of feeling safe with a person; having neither to weigh your thoughts or measure your words, but to spout them all out, as they are, chaff and grain together, knowing that a faithful friend will take them and sift them, keep what is worth keeping, and then with the breath of kindness, blow the rest away.[4]

In your time of heartbreak, leaning on true friends can help carry you through. Emerson said, "The glory of friendship is not the outstretched hand, nor the kind smile, nor the joy of companionship; it is the spiritual inspiration that comes to one when he discovers that someone else believes in him and is willing to trust him."[5] A friend is someone who knows the song in your heart and can sing it back to you when your pain has caused you to forget it. Friendship is sharing openly, laughing often, trusting always, and caring deeply. The Dave Matthews Band summed it up nicely: "I'll lean on you and you lean on me, and we'll be okay."[6]

I have found that sometimes it is hard to be the recipient of all this love. It is a humbling thing, indeed, to accept groceries from a neighbor or cash from another anonymous source. However, let me reiterate that this is what it means to be a part of the body of Christ! I pray that just like my friends rallied around me when they saw my need, I will, in turn, aid the next one who is hurting. Because really, "Jesus loves *me*, this I know for the Bible tells me so. Little ones to him belong, *we* are weak, but *he* is strong. Yes, Jesus loves *me*. Yes, Jesus loves *me*. Yes, Jesus loves *me*. The Bible tells me so." Galatians 6:9 says, "Let us not become weary in doing good, for at the proper time we will reap a harvest if we do not give up. Therefore, as we have opportunity, let us do good to all people, especially to those who belong to the family of believers." Want a friend? Be a friend! Do you see someone hurting? Be Jesus to that person.

The words of Helen Steiner Rice eloquently sum up the need we each have for a friend.

**Everyone Needs Someone**
People need people and friends need friends
And we all need love for a full life depends
Not on vast riches or great acclaim
Not on success or on worldly fame
But just in knowing that someone cares
And holds us close in their thought and prayers
For only the knowledge that we're understood
Makes every day living feel wonderfully good
And we rob ourselves of life's greatest need
When we lock up our hearts and fail to heed
The outstretched hand reaching to find
A kindred spirit whose heart and mind

Are lonely and longing to somehow share
Our joys and sorrows and to make us aware
That life's completeness and richness depends
On the things we share with our
Loved ones and friends.[7]

My friends stepped up and filled in the huge hole that was left in the wake of my husband's absence. Today there will be ample opportunities for us to help our brother or sister when we see a similar need. Another simply amazing twist to this phenomenon is watching the afflicted and hurt soul slowly begin to heal and seemingly rejoin humanity. Her smile comes back. Her laughter fills the halls once again. And as this happens, those same friends slowly, ever so slowly, reduce their aid. They gently withdraw their extended arms of support, until finally, the once flattened spirit can walk again without so much help. The goal is to see her up and flying again, soaring on wings like eagles.' And with the family of God around her and the hope of Christ within her, she can do just that!

# Letting Go

## It's a Tough Choice

I had much to be thankful for during my journey through divorce. I am all too aware that many divorces are nasty. I've seen fights over teacups and mistresses brought right into the living room to flaunt in front of the wife! I am eternally grateful that God spared me from many of those escapades. However, at some point in all splitting marriages, litigation takes place. My husband filed for divorce shortly after I filed for legal separation. In our state, the divorce cannot be finalized until sixty days after the initial filing. Those sixty days are often referred to as the litigation phase. This phase allows for hammering out all of the subsequent details of the divorce. This includes division of property, child visitation schedules, and child support regulations. Although litigation is not an emotional stage, it is superimposed on the emotional process of divorce and is primarily defined in terms of duration as a function of the legal process in your state. Generally, the process takes about one year if the divorce is fully contested in court and is considerably shorter if the parties reach an amicable agreement. Once the legal process earnestly begins, this period is characterized by the redefinition of the roles of each partner. As such, it can be either a period of tremendous growth or stagnation and despair, or it can be both, to varying degrees.[8]

The division of property is usually involved during the litigation process. This is the process of dividing all of the marital assets. For me, this was not a complicated task. Since my husband was no longer living at home and was all too caught up in other things, I took the liberty to compile a list of all of our belongings. I actually walked through every closet, each room, the basement, all storages spaces, the garage, and every nook and cranny of our house and wrote down every item or category of items that we owned. I suppose that in the back of my mind I knew I would be the primary caregiver for our children, so I had to take enough to supply a comfortable living for us. I took all of the children's furniture and about half of their toys, movies, games, etc. The other half of the toys were given to their dad for his use when the children visited him.

As for the other furniture in the house, I knew the origin of most of it, and I also knew which pieces I particularly liked and those that were my husband's favorites. I tackled the job by assessing each room and its purpose and function.

I left enough household items for my husband to effectively set up a nice home for himself without having to buy much of anything. He had a television, cookware, dinnerware, bedding, towels, etc. Why did I do this? I did it because even though he had put me through immeasurable pain, I cared about his wellbeing. I also cared about my children, who would be visiting him each week. I wanted them all to have enough to not just survive on, but to thrive on. I knew that the Lord had blessed us with plenty and I had no need for all of it. In fact, I was going to have to downsize a great deal; I simply couldn't take it all with me. It was more than I wanted to keep track of or clean.

In the end, I submitted the division of property to my husband, and he asked for one change on the list. I figured one thing wasn't too bad! I had also decided that as long as he did not try to take the children from me, he could have just about anything he wanted on the list. After all, stuff is just that—stuff. It is people that matter. I wanted to spare my relationship with him as much as possible because even though we were divorcing, I was going to be co-parenting our children with him for another fifteen years, if not longer! And so, when we had both agreed on the division of property, it was submitted to my attorney and filed with the court.

In regard to the vehicles, we owned two vans. One was an older conversion van that was paid off, and the other was a newer minivan that was years away from completely being paid off. Again, as I thought through this situation, I envisioned myself driving interstates for many miles each day with a precious cargo of children. I was about to become a single mom, and I needed a trustworthy vehicle that would not be breaking down and leaving us stranded on the road-ways. So even though there were hefty payments left to make each month, I took the newer, more reliable minivan and gave him the van that was older but already paid off.

Our house, however, was quite another matter. As I started to discover all of the details to the financial state I was in, I was horrified to learn that my name was the only name on the mortgage of our home. No matter what I wanted to do with the house, I was stuck with it. And since there was no way at all for me to make the payments on the house, I had to sit back and slowly watch it slip into foreclosure. Do you know what it feels like to be left holding the bag after the burglar got away? I do. From the very beginning, I put the house on the market. I held open houses to show the home. I watched group after group walk through, and each prospective buyer chose a different house. So what was I to do? Nothing. I had to wait. After multiple threatening phone calls from banks, I finally broke into tears on the phone with one particular debt collector. Through sobs of frustration, I was able to say, "I know I am in default of this payment. No, there is no way I can pay off the total amount due on this house. No, there is no way I can pay off the entire mortgage. I am now trying to be a single parent to four children, and I don't know what to do. Would you please stop treating me like a low-life and tell me what I should do? What would you do if you were me?" There was complete silence on the other end of the line.

Then the debt collector took a deep breath. When she started talking, the angry pit bull voice was gone and in its place was a calm, gentle, lady's voice. She sweetly replied, "Okay, I'm very sorry about your situation. I am going to go 'off the record' here and give you some personal advice. It appears that right now you still have a reasonable credit record. But after the foreclosure takes place, you will not have much of a credit score at all. So if I were you, I would go out right away and secure a different place for you and your children to live. Get arrangements made while you can. Get housing that you can afford and can keep up with the payments. As for this house, unless something else happens, it looks like it will go into foreclosure."

When I hung up the phone, I realized that Jesus himself had just spoken to me through the voice of a complete stranger who worked at a bank. Here I had been praying for wisdom about what I was supposed to do and where I was supposed to live. God had given me his wisdom. I knew what I needed to do. And so, within a couple of days, my hunt for a different home began. I figured that the five of us could manage with three bedrooms and one and one-half bathrooms. I searched the Internet, the newspaper, and spread the word everywhere I could that we needed to move as soon as possible. I looked at duplexes, townhomes, and apartments. I drove all over the city but never found the right place.

Now I suppose you are asking, "What were the qualifications for the right place?" Well, I had no energy, money, or time to devote to a large fixer-upper project. I needed something that would adequately accommodate the children and me without too much hassle. But more importantly, I was in continual prayer for God's nod of approval. What does he do for you to confirm his will to you? Does he show you specific scriptures? Does he speak wisdom through other saints? Does he speak through encouraging songs of praise? At different times of my life he has done each of these things. There is no way for me to know which way he will use to speak to me next, but I will know it when he does.

This has worked well for me. If I am not completely assured of the next step, I do not take it. So, as I looked at place after place, I could not determine the Lord's place for us; thus, I just kept looking. Finally, I found some duplexes that were relatively new and available in a small nearby town. I set up a viewing appointment and drove down by myself to take a look. When I walked through the front door of that home, I felt in my soul that sweet, gentle peace. The Lord whispered to my heart, "This is the one." Oh, yes! I had found the "right" place for us.

But what about the large, beautiful home I was leaving behind? Was God really going to let it go into foreclosure? As if I had not already been through enough, now my credit score was going to be blown to bits by a foreclosure? In the state of Kansas, a complete foreclosure cannot take place in less than four months from the time the process officially begins. The house can be sold at any time during those months, but the buyer must also agree to cover all the outstanding payments, or they must be covered by the seller. Not one prospective buyer put a bid on my home.

I was at a complete loss on this one. I had to leave it with the Lord. On one particular day I was sitting at an intersection in my town when I looked up in the sky and saw two ends of a beautiful rainbow.

*Lord,* I prayed, *if you are going to handle this house situation for me and take the burden from me, please split those clouds and let me see the whole rainbow as a promise of your faithfulness to me.* Guess what? Even as I waited for the light to turn green, the clouds parted and I saw the rainbow from one end to the other! Yes, I could leave it with him. As I drove down the street, I continued my prayer. I wanted to pray with Shadrach, Meshach, and Abednego. They showed such great trust in God. As they were about to be thrown into the fiery furnace they said to the king,

> "O Nebuchadnezzar, we do not need to defend ourselves before you in this matter. If we are thrown into the blazing furnace, the God we serve is able to save us from it, and *he will rescue us from your hand, O king. But even if he does not,* we want you to know, O king, that we will not serve your gods or worship the image of god you have set up."
>
> Daniel 3:16–18 (emphasis mine)

They were willing to burn to death, resting on the promises of God. So I prayed, *Lord, I know you have promised to take care of this house for me, but I want you to know that even if you choose not to, I will still trust you.* When I reached my destination, I shared my rainbow experience with a few of my friends, asking them to hold me accountable to my vow to leave my house in the hands of the Lord and to continue to trust him.

Waiting and trusting was no easy task. Days crawled by. No one called to look at the home; the foreclosure was in full process. The date for the auction sale of my beautiful home was set. I prayed and continued to trust. I really believed that God was going to handle this situation for me. However, when the morning of the auction arrived and my house was sold back to the bank, I was certainly puzzled. I was puzzled, not crushed. I was inquisitive, not demanding. After all, hadn't I prayed with Shadrach, Meshach, and Abednego? Didn't I trust him even if he decided not to spare my home? Well, let me remind you that our Lord sees the whole picture of our life's circumstances. His plans are far greater than we can even think or imagine!

About six and a half months after I moved out of that home and into the duplex with the children, I got a very curious phone call. The man on the other end of the line wanted to know if he could buy the redemption rights to my home. What? I told him I had absolutely no idea what he was talking about and that I no longer owned the home, as it was recently sold back to a bank through foreclosure. I was scared to discuss it further with him, so I gave him my attorney's phone number and told him he would have to talk with my attorney. Later I discovered exactly what my redemption rights were. In the state of Kansas, a person can redeem his or her home within sixty days of the foreclosure. This means that the person can, in essence, pull one's own home out of foreclosure by catching up all of the late payments. Since there was no way that I could redeem my own home, I now had other people asking to buy those redemption rights. The first offer that came in was for about one thousand dollars. Hmmm, I could profit one thousand dollars and the foreclosure would be taken off my credit record. That sounded like a great deal! But no, that was not the whole deal. After about a week, my attorney called me to express that three different people were bidding up the price of the redemption. They were up to almost seventeen thousand dollars! Oh my! In the end, my next-door neighbors bought my redemption rights and turned around and bought my home for the price of the entire first mortgage that was outstanding on it. Guess what? God came through with his rainbow promise. His timing could not have been better, but I sure didn't see that back then. He is never late, never forgetful, and never wrong.

# Other Miracles

## Our God Is So Big!

When I look back over that time in my life, I cannot help but stand in awe at so many of the wonderful things that God put together to bring about one miracle after another for me. The first was in regard to my health. Arriving almost simultaneously with the shock of divorce, I got word that I had a herniated disk in my back. Some days I was in so much pain I could hardly move. After getting three epidural shots, I scheduled my second back surgery (I had had the exact same procedure done over sixteen years before). So about a month before I moved into the duplex, I had back surgery. During the operation, several bone chips were found, the disk was shaved down, and I was cleared to resume my daily routine after about six weeks. However, now that I was single, how was I supposed to parent four kids, take care of a large home, push mow half an acre, cook meals, etc., when I would not even be walking without the aid of a walker?

Fortunately, the nature of my mother's job allowed her to come live with the children and me for weeks at a time. It was during this time that my Sunday school class got an idea. They decided to hold a moving sale for me. But this was not going to be just any old sale! They all donated their own garage sale items and combined them with all the things I was selling. The driveway of my home was at least the length of six cars, three lanes wide. On the day of the sale, tables were lined in three rows the entire length of the driveway. This took place after our division of property, so I was selling about half the things I ended up getting after the division. Then, when my friends added their things, it was more than I could comprehend.

The day of the sale dawned bright and pretty. Now I did not go out to check for certain, but it sure seemed to me that an angel had to have been standing on the corner of my street, directing traffic to my driveway. Not one time throughout that entire day did the flow of people ever let up. You need to understand this: I am a garage sale girl. I usually hold at least two garage sales every year. I try to hit as many as I can each season. I know garage/moving sales. I think making two hundred dollars from a sale is a really good sale. I would say making one hundred dollars from a garage sale made the whole thing worth the time and energy. But the sale my friends held that day for me … well, it did a little better than good. In fact, that sale brought in almost two thousand dollars! And with that money, I was able to pay off some outstanding utility bills, pay for my moving truck, and pay the down payment for the duplex. God and his people were amazing!

Another personal favorite miracle from that time came as a birthday present to me. During that same summer, I was turning thirty-something. I had no money whatsoever to spend on anything for myself for a birthday present. However, I was in the dumps emotionally. I needed to do something for myself to lift my spirits. I had no spouse to throw me a party. I had no gifts to unwrap or candles to blow out. My kids did not have any money to buy me anything, so what was I to do? Well, I looked at the checkbook and made a dumb decision. My camera had broken, and I wanted a camera to take pictures of the children. I researched local stores and found a reasonably priced digital camera. So while the children were gone one day, my mother and I headed out of the driveway to purchase a camera for me. My mom had given me her customary fifty dollars cash, so that was going to be used to help defray the cost of the $250 camera. At the foot of the driveway, however, I thought I should stop to check the mailbox for any mail.

After sifting through the usual stuff, I came upon a small white envelope with my name misspelled in childlike pencil writing. I opened the envelope and unfolded the small piece of paper. It simply read, "God provides," and into my lap fell two hundred dollars in twenty dollar bills. I started to laugh. No, I was not laughing to make fun of anything. I was laughing at the sheer goodness of a God with a sense of humor! I laughed until I cried. My mom cried right along with me. We affectionately tell people that my camera was God's gift to me for my birthday. He is an amazing God!

At this point, I want to address that person who sent me the additional cash for my camera. I have no idea who he or she is. I will probably never know! And for that, I am grateful. You see, so many people helped me in so many ways that writing the customary thank-you notes became even yet one more task for me to do. Please do not get me wrong, I wanted to thank every person who stood in the gap for me. However, there is something extra special about those gifts that were given in secret. I never put a face with those gifts. Instead, I just saw the face of God through all of his people. This was a great lesson for me to learn about giving. There will be times when I need to step up in bodily form and give. I will ring the doorbell, deliver the food, etc. However, there will be other times when I need to step back and give anonymously, simply out of obedience to God. Sometimes the hurting need to see my face, and sometimes they need to see only God working through me.

Another way this was shown was at Christmastime that first year of singleness. Again, I found myself without any money for Christmas gifts. The children would be spending the day of Thanksgiving and the day of Christmas with their father. That was just the way the holidays fell that first year. I was apprehensive about the holiday season. That is how it usually is during the first year of grief. Each major holiday, birthday, or memorable date is, to a certain extent, another date of grief. And so I was saddened that I could not make the holiday special for my children. However, God stepped up … again! My church and another local church both knew about my plight. Both churches participated in something akin to an Angel Tree ministry. The names, sizes, and wants of our family members were adopted by other families in these churches.

In the end, the children and I lacked for nothing that Christmas. We all got new clothes. We all got new toys. We had much more than I would have ever been able to buy. We had more than I was ever hoping to buy! We had enough for two or three families! Boxes of groceries covered the entire kitchen floor. God's people had once again showered us with the love of the Father. Amazing!

# Another Time of Growth

## Freedom through Forgiveness

The final stage of grief is that of growth and emergence. At this point, you understand that life will never be the same, but you accept the past and see hope and meaning in the future. You become more comfortable with who you are as a single adult and begin to think about your future. Gradually, the rollercoaster of thoughts and emotions begins to even out. Some of the intensity decreases. You begin to notice that you can make a difference in your own life, that you can create a fulfilling life for yourself after this experience. You take more action. You try new interests and discover more of your strengths and talents. You feel some fears, but you go forward in spite of them. You move from pain into possibility. You begin to let go of thoughts, beliefs, and blame that kept you locked in the past.

In this stage of growth, I learned that I have the ability to figure my own finances. I found that I could pay all the bills, collect and put the trash out at the curb on the right night, and still get up in the morning and get myself and four little people ready for each day. I slowly learned that each of the tasks that used to take two people to accomplish could be done by one, me. No, it was not my idea of fun. It was a lot of hard work. It was burning the midnight oil to keep up with laundry, clean house, write lesson plans, and still spend ample time with my children. However, since they regularly spent time visiting their dad, I had that time to catch up on grocery shopping, bill paying, and other errands. I was always tired and stressed, but I realized that, with God's help, I could handle this life I now found myself living.

One Sunday at church, while talking with a dear friend of mine who had asked me how I was doing, I responded, "I'm just waiting for things to be normal again."

He wisely responded, "Your 'normal' has been redefined. Normal for you will never be the same again. But you will figure out what your 'normal' is pretty soon." Wow! Normal is not normal. Do you follow me? Children switching houses multiple times a week will never be normal to some, but to us, that is now our definition of normal. It is not what I would like. It is not how I dreamed parenting would be. However, it is our normal.

A friend of mine has coined the phrase, "Normal is a setting on the clothes dryer." In other words, there is no such thing as normal. What is my normal today will be gone tomorrow and replaced with something new. In essence, as we age, move locations, and enter new stages of life, we constantly create new norms. The normal in my home has taken on an entirely different look, but over time, we have adequately adjusted.

By this point in my divorce, I had progressed through all the stages of grief. Someday, you will look back only to discover that you too have made it through all of these same stages. However, it is important to realize that the stages can overlap. You can be in more than one stage at the same time and can also regress into previous stages. Obviously, if you were crushed over the sadness of your divorce, you will probably handle these stages differently than a person who was content and happy to move on with her life. In addition to the predictable stages, there are predictable emotions, fears, and feelings. These include rejection (the most basic, universal feeling for the non-initiator), anger, loneliness, confusion, self-doubt, depression, the fear of making mistakes, the fear of being inadequate, the fear of going over the edge, anxiety over the unknown, self-pity, and believe it or not, euphoria.[1]

Even as we will circle back around, in and out of these stages of grief, we will also move in and out of the various emotions, fears, and feelings. However, the greatest component for helping me maintain a level sense of emotional rightness was the not-so-simple act of forgiveness. There is an old saying that he who angers you controls you. I have found that to be absolutely true. My ex-husband continually does things that anger me. My friends or co-workers or students do things that upset me. However, it is in clinging to those things and seeking to right the wrong that I find myself in a miserable state.

University of Michigan psychologist Christopher Peterson said that the ability to forgive others is the trait most strongly linked to happiness. He calls the ability to forgive others "the queen of all virtues, and probably the hardest to come by."[2] Furthermore, studies by a number of psychologists show that it is not great riches that make people happy, but friends and forgiveness.

How exactly do you go about forgiving the person who has done nothing short of demolish your entire life? In one fell swoop, your cheating spouse took your world and jerked the rug right out from underneath it, leaving you to pick up the pieces of what little was left after it all came crashing down. Forgive? Is that really possible? The way I see it, I chose to forgive my ex-husband for two specific purposes. The first is beautifully explained by Stephen Arterburn.

> The reason for forgiveness is not to let the other person off the hook; it is to get you unhooked. You forgive so you can move on. Every moment spent in holding a grudge keeps you trapped in the event that took place too long ago for you to be holding on. When you choose to forgive, you are not freeing the other person; you are freeing yourself.[3]

In essence, by hanging on to anger, resentment, and hurt, I only kept myself bound to my husband. I just wanted to get even or to hurt him as much as he hurt me.

Is this how Christ Jesus offers us forgiveness? No! When Jesus was hanging on the cross after being beaten beyond belief, he said, "Father, forgive them, for they do not know what they are doing" (Luke 23:34). And in the instant that I cry out for mercy, Jesus wipes my slate clean, remembering my sins no more. So you ask, "What if my spouse doesn't repent?" or "What if my spouse never asks for forgiveness?" That doesn't matter. According to this first reason for forgiveness, you forgive for yourself. You free yourself from bitterness. You move on because you are free to do so. There is no longer a get-even attitude.

Let me say here that I really struggled with the concept of true forgiveness. I sought godly counsel on this exact point. In my personal walk with Christ, I desired to completely forgive my husband. But I wondered if true forgiveness was the same as reconciliation. In other words, if my husband confessed, apologized, and made efforts to change his ways, if true forgiveness were applied, would I have to take my husband back and resume our previous relationship exactly as it had been? Please understand that my husband did confess, did apologize, and did make some effort to change his ways. However, his efforts were never about pleasing God or even about pleasing me. He continued to want to live a double life. At this juncture, I heard someone say that true forgiveness is when you no longer wish ill will on someone. In fact, it is when you pray for that person to be all that he can be in Christ.

You move from a "hurt spouse" position to a "brother or sister in Christ" position. You only want good things for the person who hurt you so badly. However, those good things do not necessarily involve you.

In the deepest part of your soul, do you want your spouse to suffer some of what you had to go through? Do you want to see him crawl to you, begging for forgiveness? Do you want to give him a taste of what he gave you? If so, you have not reached the point of true forgiveness. In fact, most of the time the cheating spouse either doesn't know all that he has done to you, or he simply does not care. It is likely that he will never know the full extent of the pain he has caused you. Even if he were to some-day remarry and his new spouse cheated on him, he still would not understand all the hurt he caused. It is time, therefore, to stop looking for him to come crawling up to your doorstep. It is time to stop waiting for him to hum-bly confess on bended knee, pleading for your forgiveness. Rather, it is simply time to lay it down. And what is "lay it down?" you ask. It is my mantra for getting through the things I do not see as fair.

Each time you lay it down, you say to the Father, "God, I don't know why this is happening to me, and it hurts so much. I am so mad at the unfairness. Honestly, there is a part of me that wants to get even. But that is only my humanness. What I want most of all is to trust you. I do trust you. You promised that your eye is always on the righteous. You promised that you are a God of wrath and a jealous God. I want to leave the get-even part to you. I want to be free to move on with my life. I want to be free from bitterness, hatred, and ill will. Please take this specific hurt and cover it with the same love that you showed when you died on this cross for my sin. I commit to leave this hurt here with you. I trust you to help me move on."

As I continued to learn to lay it down, I also learned that it is possible to completely forgive that person without reinstating the previous relationship. It is possible to love your cheating spouse as a brother in Christ rather than as a marriage partner. Ephesians 4:32 says, "Be kind and compassionate to one another, forgiving each other, just as in Christ God forgave you." It is possible to be kind and compassionate to the one who crushed your feelings. It is possible to forgive him. With God's help, forgiveness can be extended to the vilest offender.

I knew that I would need to guard against bitterness, anger, pride, and even hate. I have been around people that reminded me of porcupines. They were so bristly that I cringed to spend much time with them. They seemed to walk around with a dark storm cloud hovering over their heads twenty-four hours a day. They were in an ongoing battle with God or others, and they were not willing to let God rain down peace on their very souls. One morning as I stood in the shower with the hot water beating down on the top of my head, I prayed that the water would literally be a covering of protection for me that day. I prayed against any darts that Satan might hurl. I prayed against any lies I might hear. I prayed against hurt that would cut deeply. I prayed that water be a symbolic yet spiritual covering over my entire body that day. I prayed for God's peace to cover me completely. And guess what?

God is faithful! I have felt that peace every day since then. I can rest assured, knowing that God has a plan that is far grander than anything I could dream up, and there is a vast amount of peace knowing that!

In her book *The Hiding Place*, Corrie Ten Boom vividly recalls all the events leading up to and including the arrest and imprisonment of her family in Nazi Germany during WWII. After watching her sister, Betsie, die at Ravensbruck, one of the prison camps, Corrie survived and preached the gospel when the war was over.

The following is Corrie's wonderful example of living, true forgiveness:

> It was at a church service in Munich that I saw him, the former S.S. man who had stood guard at the shower room door in the processing center at Ravensbruck. He was the first of our actual jailers that I had seen since that time. And suddenly it was all there—the roomful of mocking men, the heaps of clothing, Betsie's pain-blanched face.
>
> He came up to me as the church was emptying, beaming and bowing. "How grateful I am for your message, Fräulein," he said. "To think that, as you say, he has washed my sins away!"
>
> His hand was thrust out to shake mine. And I, who had preached so often to the people in Bloementdaal the need to forgive, kept my hand at my side.
>
> Even as the angry, vengeful thoughts boiled through me, I saw the sin of them. Jesus Christ had died for this man; was I going to ask for more?

Lord Jesus, I prayed, forgive me and help me to forgive him.

I tried to smile. I struggled to raise my hand. I could not. I felt nothing, not the slightest spark of warmth or charity. And so again I breathed a silent prayer. Jesus, I cannot forgive him. Give me your forgiveness.

As I took his hand the most incredible thing happened. From my shoulder along my arm and through my hand a current seemed to pass from me to him, while into my heart sprang a love for this stranger that almost overwhelmed me.

And so I discovered that it is not on our forgiveness any more than on our goodness that the world's healing hinges, but on his. When he tells us to love our enemies, he gives, along with the command, the love itself.[4]

Corrie's example also sheds light on the second reason I believe we are to truly forgive. Mark Twain once said, "Forgiveness is the fragrance the rose shed on the heel that has crushed it." Interpretation? Even though you were the one that was crushed, you can still be Jesus to the one who hurt you. Corrie traveled around preaching the gospel. She lived her life to draw others to Christ. Isn't that what we want to do each day with our lives? We may not necessarily be called to preach and travel from post to post, but we are all called to share the good news. Who needs to hear the good news more than those lost in sin? Jesus said, "I have not come to call the righteous, but sinners" (Matthew 9:13b). How will they know about the love of Jesus if we do not tell them and if we do not show them?

Chuck Swindoll once said, "Life is ten percent what happens to us and ninety percent how we react to it. Our attitude towards things is more important than the things themselves."[5] In our case, our attitude toward our wayward spouses is more important than the sins they committed. Perhaps through our life of Christian love and forgiveness, we can be the one to shed light on the path for others who are coming behind us. Oswald Chambers put it this way: "If you will receive yourself in the fires of sorrow, God will make you nourishment for other people."[6] For example, within just a few months of my divorce, I was able to help counsel two other women who found themselves in similar situations. No, I did not have all the right answers for them. Their particular situations were not the same as mine. However, I was traveling that road of rejection just ahead of them. I knew enough to share a few things, and even a few things can help another person in need. Unforgiveness puts an abrupt stop to growth in Jesus. We are bound to the person we will not forgive and then hung up on bitterness so that we cannot break free. Our choice to forgive frees us from bitterness and begins our healing. Our act of forgiveness can also be a light for our wayward spouse and even an example for others to follow. When you truly forgive, it is a beautiful thing. Can you work toward forgiving your wayward spouse and even yourself if need be?

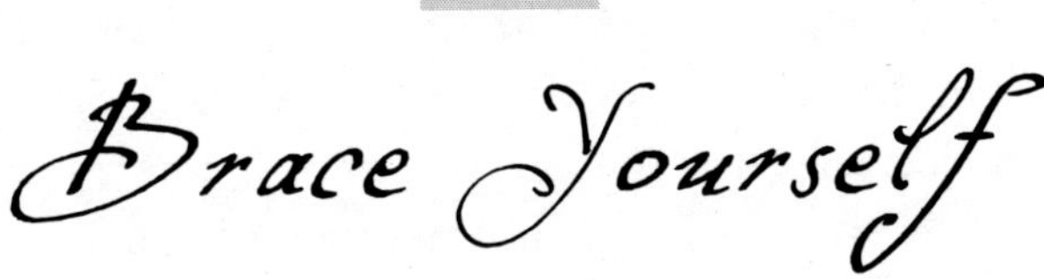

# Brace Yourself

## Be Dressed for Battle

We do not really struggle against people, whether that is misbehaving children, wayward spouses, or lousy bosses. Rather, our battle is against Satan and the sin that comes into the lives of otherwise good people. For this reason, it will be necessary at times to take the huge *why* question and simply set it aside. We may never have an adequate answer for that question. If we get hung up on a pursuit for the answer, we may altogether miss the precious lessons to be learned along the way and the opportunities for growth with Jesus.

Put on the armor "so that when the day of evil comes, you may be able to stand your ground" (Ephesians 6:13). This verse does not say *if* a day of evil comes. Instead, it says *when* the day of evil comes. I believe that each one of us will face trials that seem impossible. We will find ourselves at the end our ropes, scared, completely frustrated, or all of the above. However, it is at our wits' end that we will find God.

The key here is to put on the full armor of God before your day of evil hits. Picture this: It is the middle of the battle. Your enemy is rushing toward you, sword brandished, ready to strike. All of a sudden, you put up your hands in the well-known "T" formation to call a time-out so that you can get dressed in your armor before resuming the battle. No, no! This is not the way it is done in the movies or real life! Your armor has to be on well before you are even aware of what form of evil will come against you. Do not wait for the death of a loved one, the loss of a job, the news of infertility or divorce to hit before you realize your need to be clothed in armor. At that point it is much harder to get properly "dressed." However, knowing that you are probably already deep in the battle, hang on and learn what to do to be victorious!

Put on the armor "so that when the day of evil comes, you may be able to stand your ground, and after you have done everything, to stand" (Ephesians 6:13). A few years ago we lived in Florida. We were there for four nasty hurricanes. During those storms, it was fascinating to watch the trees. Palm trees do not have a very deep root system but are highly flexible with thin, long trunks. When the winds picked up to 110 mph, the palms bent low to the ground but rarely snapped, and the next day, after the winds calmed, the palm trees were standing tall. For the other trees that appeared taller and had thicker and tougher trunks, this was just not so. These trees had extensive root systems in the sandy soil, and they had little or no give in their trunks. When the high winds hit those trees, one of two things often happened. First, some would bend as much as possible until finally they would snap in two, giving the appearance of an upright pencil broken in half. Others were thick in the trunk and so heavy that the winds literally ripped the trees and their entire root systems out of the ground, uprooting the massive, gorgeous trees.

From this analogy, we can see that to withstand the storm, the palm trees had to have a circuit of roots and a flexible trunk. These trees had their armor on before the storm hit. Even though the storm hit every tree and the palms were bent low in the thrashing winds, their armor saved them in the end and they were able to get back up and once again stand tall. Guess what? No matter where your circumstances find you today, you too can get back up and stand tall.

"Stand firm then, with the belt of truth buckled around your waist, with the breastplate of righteousness in place" (Ephesians 6:14). I always think of righteousness as *right* living. It is thinking of the WWJD (What Would Jesus Do) concept. If we are in the Word and living in the Light of Truth, we will know how to make choices like Jesus would, always putting others before ourselves, taking up our crosses, and laying down our lives. Isaiah 45:19 says, "I, the Lord, speak the truth; I declare what is right." In difficult times when so many people want to help us with their kind words of advice, we must be sure to line up our thoughts and decisions with the Word of the Lord. Only his ways are truly right.

Paul knew about the godlessness of people, even in his time. Or was it that he knew what life would be like with each passing generation? In 2 Timothy 3:1–7, we read of our own society:

> But mark this: There will be terrible times in the last days. People will be lovers of themselves, lovers of money, boastful, proud, disobedient to their parents, ungrateful, unholy, without love, unforgiving, slanderous, without self-control, brutal, not lovers of the good, treacherous, rash, conceited, lovers of pleasure rather than lovers of God—have a form of godliness but denying its power. Have nothing to do with them. They are the kind who worm their way into homes and gain control over weak-willed women, who are loaded down with sins and are swayed by all kinds of evil desires, always learning but never able to acknowledge the truth.

Let's not live like this! May those who come behind us find us faithful to the cross of Christ! May they find us focused on loving him and loving others. May we continually seek the truth of the Father who brings life everlasting.

And so we must also put on the shoes of readiness that comes from the gospel of peace. "The Lord gives strength to his people; the Lord blesses his people with peace" (Ephesians 6:15). Before Jesus left this world, he gave us the Holy Spirit, the Counselor. He gave us his peace so that we would not be troubled or afraid (John

14:25–27). Finally, Philippians 4:7 says, "And the peace of God, which transcends all understanding will guard your hearts and your minds in Christ Jesus."

Deuteronomy 6:5–9 says,

> Love the Lord your God with all your heart and with all your soul and with all your strength. These commandments that I give you today are to be upon your hearts. Impress them on your children. Talk about them when you sit at home and when you walk along the road, when you lie down and when you get up. Tie them as symbols on your hands and bind them on your foreheads. Write them on the doorframes of your houses and on your gates.

Since walking around with prayers and commands written on our foreheads might not be very effective today, I chose to write them in a prayer journal. I once read that rather than struggling with what to read from Scripture each day during quiet time, why not try to read a portion of Scripture and stop when any one verse or thought jumped out at me. Then write that one insight in my journal and spend some time writing and reflecting on how or why that verse applied to me. Then pray about that new knowledge. Do not resume reading any more Scripture at that time. Spend that day in reflection of that verse. I love this principle! Some days I read three chapters before something hits me. Other days I read three verses. Either way, I begin my reading by asking God to show me what he wants for me that day, that hour, that moment.

It is proven and backed by the medical field that writing out our feelings, frustrations, and losses is therapeutic. In their counseling session for separated and divorced parents, representatives from my state even suggested that this helps heal divorced families quicker. But one of the neatest parts of journaling is that as I go back and read what I wrote several days or months ago, I often cannot remember what I was dealing with concerning that particular issue. My perspective has changed, and I get to see a timeline of how miraculously God was present and working in that very situation, although at that time I could not see it. Journaling is a way of keeping documentation of God's faithfulness.

Put on the armor, the helmet of salvation. "The Lord is my strength and my song; he has become my salvation" (Exodus 15:2). Psalm 27:1 beautifully says, "The Lord is my light and my salvation—whom shall I fear? The Lord is the stronghold of my life—of whom shall I be afraid?" He is our rock! He is our fortress and deliverer (Psalm 62:2)! There is no other person, force, thing, or entity that can bring salvation. Only through Jesus Christ are we eternally saved (Acts 4:12). Do you know him today as your personal Savior? Do you want to be rescued from the pit of sin you find yourself wallowing in? Why not ask him to forgive you of all of your sins and watch him make you into a brand-new person? All you need to do is pray, acknowledging your need for a Savior and asking him to forgive your sins. Then commit your life to him. It is as easy as ABC: admit, believe, and commit. I would then suggest that you contact a pastor and tell him of your decision to follow Christ. He will be able to further counsel you in your new walk with Christ. By the way, if you are already a believer in Christ, see how simple it really is to lead someone to the Lord? Why are we afraid to share the gospel? After all, it is the best news ever!

And so we must also put on the armor of the sword of the spirit, the Word of God (Ephesians 6:17). The Word of God often sits on the bookshelf, collecting dust. Many of our homes boast a collection of several copies, yet none are frequently read. This is a terrible problem even in the homes of many Christians. How are we to know the Lord's precepts and principles if we don't chisel out time to read his Word each day? Are we saying that our earthly friends, families, and agendas are more important than our relationship with Jesus? Speaking for myself, I don't believe that we intentionally set out to become too busy for Jesus. Our daily lives just tend to get so full of so many otherwise good things that we inadvertently squeeze Jesus into three-second wish prayers. However, truly growing in relationship with Jesus only comes through investment in him. Deuteronomy 8:3 says, "Man does not live on bread alone but on every word that comes from the mouth of the Lord." And where do we hear his words? In the Holy Scriptures. It is only through the reading of God's Word that you fully realize all that embodies the person that God wants you to be.-And then we must put on the armor by praying in the Spirit on all occasions (Ephesians 6:18).

There is nothing wrong with presenting our prayers and petitions to the Lord, even in full detail of how we would like to see them turn out. However, I do believe that God knows what is truly in our best interest, and it is a good thing that we don't always get what we prayed for! I pray for myself, for those close to me, and even for the most minute details of life. I believe God cares for every aspect of my being. After all, Christ is living in me. I endeavor to walk in step with his Holy Spirit as my guide. Praying for God's will, hoping for a certain outcome, but always accepting God's answer is the way I choose to go.

So finally, we need to put on the armor by praying for the saints. We need to lift up one another's burdens to the Lord. Are you standing in the gap for those who are hurting in the body of Christ? Prayer changes things. If nothing else, prayer changes the one who is actually doing the praying. It is hard to pray for the lost without feeling a sense of compassion for them. Likewise, it is hard to pray for your wayward spouse without realizing his need for a savior. It is hard to pray earnestly for him to find the Lord while you are calling him an idiot. Do you see what I mean? If we are out of sorts with someone at our church, perhaps we should get down on our knees and pray for that dear lady. By doing so, we acknowledge that she too is a beloved child of God, in need of forgiveness and friendship. Perhaps we can begin to see the situation through her eyes, instead of just our own.

In conclusion, Chambers says,

> We do not always know what God's compelling purpose is, but whatever happens, we must maintain our relationship with him. The most important aspect of Christianity is not the work we do, but the relationship we maintain and the surrounding influence and qualities produced by that

relationship. That is all God asks us to give our attention to, and it is the one thing that is continually under attack.[1]

So put on the full armor of God so that when your day of evil comes, you will be equipped to stand.

# You're Still Human

## The Pain Still Hurts

Knowing all of the pieces of the armor of God will help us face our battles. However, it is dangerous to forget that we are human beings. We are hurt. We need help. We don't have the bird's-eye view like God does. We can only see this one moment in time, and from this perspective, things are bad, really bad. So what do you do? Do you remember seeing movies or seeing the news broadcasts of those people who are going through gut-wrenching pain? Could you see the anguish on their faces? Was it hard for you to watch them in their pain?

I have a dear friend whose mother died of breast cancer.

My friend Julie took care of her mother in her last days. A few years after her mother's death, I asked Julie what those dying moments were like. Julie replied, "I was sitting on my bed with my mother in my arms. Hospice had visited several times, and I knew it was getting close to the end. When she breathed her last breath, I was crushed. I screamed out to Jim. And the very next thing I knew, I was wailing. I don't mean crying. I mean wailing. I cried out to God. I just let it all out. It was the most amazingly healing thing I could do at that moment."

So, friend, have you cried out to Jesus? I don't mean cried; I mean wailed. I have. Sometimes the grief overtakes me in an instant. Sometimes I just need to get on the floor and weep before the Lord. Sometimes I need to wail so loud and so long that I have nothing left. I need to be absolutely physically and emotionally spent before the Lord. And you know what? He always meets me there. One such instance was the night of my move from the nice lush, big house to the duplex. I was all alone, driving the keys for the moving truck over to a friend's house so that he could drive the truck the next day. I was about a block from his house when it hit me. I pulled my van over to the side of the road as fear gripped my heart. *I can't do this! I can't start over all by myself! I don't know what I'm doing. I can't raise these kids alone!* I wept and cried out to God. It was physical, emotional, spiritual, all of me. In that instant, the CD in my car hit the old great song "Because He Lives," the chorus of which is: "Because he lives, I can face tomorrow. Because he lives, all fear is gone. Because I know he holds the future and life is worth the living, just because he lives."[1]

Okay, so God met me right then. When I heard those words, I started laughing. God knew right where I was. He knew I was scared to take one more step. However, he also knew that I needed a gentle reminder that I could go on because he was going with me!

Another time I remember wailing before the Lord was when I was at home in the duplex, all alone. I had just watched the kids pull out of the driveway for a long weekend with their dad. My home sounded so quiet, it seemed like a tomb. I did not want to be alone! I had not carried four kids for nine months each in my womb and raised them all to this point for me to now find myself in the living room of my home, all quiet and alone. Once again, I popped in a CD, and the song "In Christ Alone" started to play. As the words broke the silence, I started to break down before the Father. I was physically all the way down. I was on the floor, facedown, wailing out my misery to God.

One of my former pastors once said that it is "okay to kick God in the shins because he can take it." When I first heard that, I thought it was terribly sacrilegious. However, I now think I understand what he was saying. God already knows our pain. In fact, he feels it right along with us. He laughs when we laugh, and he cries when we cry. So it is okay to be completely real before him. That is what he wants. And it is in those times that we truly acknowledge our need for a deliverer.

Even my two-year-old son was wise enough to know that Mom had had all she could take the day I locked myself in the bathroom and started wailing. He shot out of my room, up the stairs, and down the hall to inform his sisters that

"Mummy cwying!" He said it over and over. The next thing I heard were the running footsteps of the girls heading straight for the bathroom door. They needed to know that I was okay. They needed to hear me reassure them. I just needed a little more time to share with God how frustrated and hurt I was. I assured the children that I was fine but that I needed a break and that I would be out of the bathroom in a few minutes. They camped outside the door until they could see my face, but at least I knew they were concerned for me. That time, God sent my kids to show me that they needed me and loved me, and they were a huge reason to keep fighting the good fight and keep going.

Another time I was driving down the road near a local superstore, with tears streaming down my face. I was worn out. I didn't think I could take one more minute of my life. Then right before my eyes flashed a scene of the old rugged cross. On it hung my Lord, all beaten and battered. The Holy Spirit whispered to me, "I could have stopped that too." It hit me like a punch in the stomach. God let Jesus suffer more than I could even imagine so that I could truly live. Now I was living in a nightmare, but God was allowing that too, for a much better cause. Yes, he could stop the madness in my life, or he could allow it in order to help me grow into the person he really needed and wanted me to be. My life could be a living example for others to follow. How would I handle adversity? Would I cave and rant and rave that no truly loving God would let such bad things happen to good people? God allows bad things to happen because we live in a fallen world. Sin is all around us, and we will be touched by its tentacles, whether we are the sinners or those affected by the sins of others. Until we get to heaven, we will be in this world of sin, but not of it. We are covered by the blood of Jesus. Heaven is our real home. "And a highway will be there; it will be called the Way of Holiness. The unclean will not journey on it; it will be for those who walk in the Way" (Isaiah 35:8). Right now, we are just passing through this world. Our time here is short, but we want to live it all for him.

At one point in the *Love Comes Softly* movie series, one of the lead characters, Marty, has lost her husband and finds herself alone, pregnant, and now married to a complete stranger. She wails while swinging. She cries herself to sleep. Then Clarke, her new husband, and Missie, his little girl, come to Marty's bedroom door to check on her. Missie asks Clarke if Marty is okay. Clarke responds, "No, but she will be." That is exactly how I felt for many, many months. Was I okay? No. Was I going to be okay? Yes. We are human. We take things slow and easy. In matters of the heart, time does heal. For some, it takes months to work through the pain of rejection. For some it takes years. However, I believe that all of us who have been rejected by another human being will never be the same again. We have been through the deep waters and the valley of the shadow of death. We will never casually approach another human relationship.

When my sister-in-law heard of all that had happened in my marriage, she commented that under the same circumstances it would have been easier on her if my brother had suddenly died rather than reject her. Dobson said the same thing. "Death itself would be easier to tolerate than being tossed aside like an old shoe. Those who have experienced such a loss tell me that the most painful aspect is their own loneliness."[2] The death of a spouse does not usually come by choice. If he died in a car accident or of a heart attack, he didn't choose to disregard your feelings and tear your family apart. When a spouse has an affair, files for divorce, and walks away from something that was beautiful, he chose it. He chose something else over you. And that hurts. That cuts to the core. That shakes the foundations of all that is good and right.

This brings us to the concept of submission. What does it mean for a toddler to submit to his dad when they are approaching an intersection in the road and his dad yells "Stop!"? Does it mean, "Wait right there while I explain to you why you need to look both directions? A car might be coming, so let me teach you how to check for traffic"? No! A toddler that truly submits to his dad's authority simply stops walking and waits for the go-ahead from his dad because he knows that he can trust his dad to do what is right. So let's look at our lives. Do we trust our heavenly Father? Do we know that what he is doing is right? Yes! So what does our submission to his authority really look like?

First, it does not look like the blame game. It does not look like anger toward God, our spouse, our family members, or even the situation. It does not embody pointing the finger at the reasons why things happened. Next, it does not look like the prove-it method. We cannot barter with the Lord and come out the winner. We cannot play the "If you do this, then I'll do that" relationship. Simply put, Jesus already did all that needed to be done when he died in our place as a sacrifice for our sins on the cross. His part is done. Now he wants us to do our part and trust him, pure and simple. When we have the Holy Spirit within us, we have the ability to be aware of things that are not otherwise obvious. Sometimes we just need to pull ourselves up by our bootstraps, so to speak, and tell ourselves to stop. If we listen to the Holy Spirit, he will be our guide. We can submit to the Lord's ultimate authority and keep in step with the Spirit. "Strengthen the feeble hands, steady the knees that give way, say to those with fearful hearts, 'Be strong, do not fear; your God will come, he will come with vengeance; with divine retribution he will come to save you'" (Isaiah 35:3–5).

# Moving On

## Stepping Back into the Dating Scene

Statistics indicate that fifty percent of all first marriages fail, but are you aware the divorce rates of second marriages are estimated to be over seventy percent? Maybe this explains why many people end up married three and four times before they find that person to grow old and live with until "death do us part."[1]

So how exactly are you supposed to move on when you thought you had already married your for-life spouse? You do not have to live the rest of your life alone, but there are some heavy precautions that one must consider before making the leap back into the dating scene.

First, you don't ever want to start dating just because you are lonely. Of course you are lonely! Each of us that has been rejected faces terrible nights of loneliness. Sitting by yourself in front of the television eating bonbons and thinking about your former spouse in the arms of another person is enough to drive anyone batty! However, loneliness simply cannot drive us into the arms of a new person. If we give in to that desire, we will find ourselves broken again, and often, we will break the hearts of others in the process. The cure to loneliness at this stage in the game needs to be found in one's friends and family. Did you know it can take many months to get used to going out with a group of friends when you're single? You carry around in your head this idea that most of your friends will say good-bye at the end of the evening and go home to the nice, warm bed their spouse is sleeping in. You'll head home to chilly, lonely sheets.

It took me several months to realize deep within myself that I was truly single again. It had been almost seventeen years since I had been alone. All that time I had a significant other in my life. Whether I realized it or not, all those years I carried thoughts, concerns, and plans for that relationship and that man. When I went to the grocery store I thought, *What would he like for dinner tomorrow night?* When I painted the bedroom I wondered, *Will he like this color?* No matter where I went and what I did, I always carried my spouse with me, in both my head and my heart. So when I found myself once again a single, I had to find my place in the world all over again.

One day I called a pastor at my church and asked if he

would meet with me. This pastor had been at our church for many years. He had counseled several couples whose marriages were in trouble. He had seen some mend and restore their relationships, and he had watched many others fall apart despite his efforts to help. My marriage was already lost at that point, but I really needed to talk through my feelings of loneliness and my desire to move on with my life. I felt like a wounded animal caught by one leg in a trap. I could not pull that remaining part away from my past in order to be free to bound into my future. I wondered if it was okay to get back out there again. Could I really go on a date? Could I really share a table for two with someone other than my former spouse? How exactly does a person do that? At first, it feels so very wrong! My friend Sheila had this to say about reentering the dating scene: "I hated it. I didn't want to be a part of it. It was a scary place. I was fearful about how to start over. It is an incredibly lonely place."

Reverend Tony Evans wrote a book entitled *Single and Satisfied*. My friend Sheila found that book to be very helpful to her in her journey through singlehood. She and I both agreed that until you are at peace with being single, you are not ready to join the dating world. A young lady at my church approached me recently with tears in her eyes. She said that I was an inspiration to her and that she would like to tell me her story. She began by telling me that she had just turned thirty and did not want to live any longer since God had not brought a man into her life. Yikes! That is a real problem. As I see it, God will not bring the right person into your life until you have found your sense of belonging in Jesus Christ. We do not exist on this planet for any other reason than to bring glory to God. If we move through each day living in the dumps because we do not have the human relationship we want, we are missing the entire point of our existence!

My pastor pointed out that Matthew 6:33–34 says, "But seek first his kingdom and his righteousness and all these things will be given to you as well. Therefore do not worry about tomorrow, for tomorrow will worry about itself. Each day has enough trouble of its own." I used to read that verse and interpret the first part as, "Tell God what you need and then he will give it to you." No, no, no! It actually means, "Get to know God. Learn about him. Study his Word and his ways. Learn from the Word how you fit into his plan. Seek righteousness. Seek right living." In essence, fall in love with Jesus. He is all you will ever need. Once you have worked through that step and keep practicing it each day, the Lord will give to you what you need. Perhaps you do need another spouse. Maybe you don't. Maybe you need a great circle of friends or one very good friend. Maybe you need to rechannel your energies to aid the kingdom in a new and different way by taking on a new ministry. Whatever the case may be, if you are living for Jesus, you will grow to be satisfied in him.

I came away from meeting with my pastor having learned some important lessons. It is okay to be scared. We are in an entirely new place. We are out of our element, and we have been burned so badly that we are afraid to put our necks out there again for fear our heads will be chopped off, not to mention our very hearts have been torn out and have been stomped all over! These feelings are all normal. For this reason, we don't want to rush ahead without great caution. Also, I came to realize that it would be possible to love a man other than my former spouse. A friend of mine reminded me of my own four children. When I only had one, I thought there was no way I could love another as much as I loved that first daughter. Then I had my second daughter. It didn't mean I loved my first daughter any less. It just meant that I was able to grow room in my heart and love them both equally, yet in different ways since each one is a unique creation of God. And so, even though I had loved my first spouse with all that was in me and I had devoted my life to him, I could now turn around and offer those same things to another man if the Lord sent one to me.

How long should one wait to start dating again? One year? (No, you don't have to wear black for one year!) My own counselor offered that he thought women should wait at least two to three years after a divorce and men should wait three to five. I could get into all the details of those differing time frames, but I will leave that to those with the medical/psychological degrees. Another number I heard thrown around several times was an equation. It stated that you need to give yourself two months for every year you were married. Calculated out in this way, since I was married for fourteen and one-fourth years, I *should have* waited to date for two and one-fourth years. Okay, but was I supposed to count from the date of the official court-ruled divorce or from the time my husband last slept with me in my bed? There were several months between those times that I was alone. My point here is:

do not put God in a box, or an equation, for that matter. If you seek true healing and guidance from the Father, he will always show up on time for you. If he brings another person into your life, his timing is always right, no matter if it is two years or sixteen.

"The critical issue is not when you remarry," writes Barbara Lovenheim in *Beating the Marriage Odds*, "but why you remarry and whom you select as a spouse…If you give yourself time to know who you are and what you want and what you can offer to a spouse, your chances of creating a solid marriage are enhanced."[2] Again, I don't think there is a magic number of years or months to wait until starting to date again. I believe that if you rely solely on the Holy Spirit as your guide, he will steer you correctly every time (even when it may not seem like it to others around you).

In preparation for reentry to the dating world, Dr. De Angelis says, "The first thing you should do is a deep assessment of your first marriage and earlier relationships. How did they function? What didn't work? Were there problems with sex, or power struggles? You then have to reevaluate yourself, work on yourself."[3] Before considering remarriage, make sure that it is really what you want. Remember, it is better to be single and independent than to compromise your beliefs, values, and goals for the sake of being in a relationship.

Caution should be used whenever meeting or communicating with a new person. For example, when sharing information with a new "friend" online, never give out your address, phone number, or any other pertinent information until you are absolutely sure you are ready to trust that person with such information. Remember the old adage "Don't believe everything you hear"? Well, in the case of meeting people online, don't believe everything you read either. Even well-meaning people will try to make themselves look and sound good in an effort to impress the reader on the other end of the message.

Another way to proceed with caution is to make sure you have adequately processed through each of the stages of grief from your divorce. Yes, you will find yourself circling back through some of those stages for years to come, but it is important to allow yourself ample time to grieve the loss of one relationship before entering another one. When you have prayed it through and find yourself ready to put your baby toe in the kiddie pool of dating, perhaps the best way to start is through group activities. Many churches offer a singles group or Sunday school class where nearly every person in the room is single. In that aspect, each person has a point of connection. Each one understands loneliness, but hopefully each one has also learned to love God and his plan for his or her life.

Attending a social activity with a group of singles does not mean that you are throwing yourself out there like a piece of raw meat for all the people of the opposite sex to gawk over. Rather, a well-run program will plan activities where each person can find a place of acceptance in a group. The activities are intended to bring people together and provide an evening of fun. It does not have to be a divorcees anonymous meeting or an "I'll tell my nightmare, then you tell yours" type of event. The neat thing about this environment is that it enables many singles to create important friendships with other singles of the same sex and the opposite.

Dating the second time around is much different than it was when you were in your teenage years. Back then, you were super-duper impressed with the handsome guy who lived down the street. However, after being rejected once, most of us do not want just any cute guy who lives down the street. In fact, we know exactly what we do want, or at least what we think we need. The first thing you should not look for is someone with many similar characteristics of your former spouse. Don't go looking for a remake of what you just lost. That is a sign that you are not ready to give any other person a fair chance to establish a relationship with you.

Another thing you should not do is look for someone on whom to unload your burdens. Yes, at some point I am sure both of you will share the gory details of your hurtful pasts, but when looking for the right person, look for someone with whom you can be happy. Does he make you laugh? Do you enjoy leaving your problems behind as you find new joy in this unique person? Are you excited to be with him? Remember, it is okay to have fun again. If you find that you simply cannot laugh and have fun, then you are not ready to be in the dating world again. More healing needs to take place. And until that happens, it would be better for you to stick with group activities.

Group activities also allow you to get to know someone as a friend before deciding to date that person. Again, this can be done in a singles ministry at church, or it can simply be a person you have already known for some time but never looked at as a possible date because you were committed to another person. In reaching out to familiarize yourself with another person, don't be fake. Be yourself. Hopefully this will give him permission to do the same. Don't play games with facades. Take off the masks and be real with each other and the others in your group. Have fun sharing in life's times of joy and friendship. Soon, if you enjoy being in each other's company, you will find yourself spending more and more time together.

My own story does not fit the cookie-cutter equation or plan that most psychologists would counsel. I will not make excuses for what happened in my life. I can only say that it was a miracle of God. I had been attending my church for almost sixteen years and knew most of the folks that attended our congregation of over seven hundred. I did not live near any of my family, so people in my church rallied around and supported me. One such person was Mike. Shortly after I moved into my duplex, he caught me at church and offered to bring a meal over for the kids and me. I asked if he could also stay and help put together the trampoline for the children. So on a beastly hot night in July, Mike showed up with dinner and stayed to sweat buckets putting together the trampoline. I thanked him and told him I would be seeing him at church. Before he left that night, he simply said, "I live here in town, nearby, so if you need anything, be sure to let me know." Again I thanked him and watched him close the door.

Just a few days later, I found out that my entire oven and range would not work. I remembered Mike's offer and called him for help. When he arrived he pulled out my stove to find that it simply was not plugged in. I felt so dumb!

Why hadn't I thought of that? But I am no expert on these things. In fact, I generally want to hyperventilate when I am in a home improvement store. I thanked Mike profusely and thanked God for helping me out of this bind.

Some days after that, the children (along with an additional one) were enjoying ice cream in the kitchen. One of my daughters dropped her bowl on the kitchen floor, and, of course, it broke. I picked up all the pieces and went to scoop up the ice cream off the floor, when a large shard of glass cut right into my unsuspecting thumb. I am no nurse, but when something bleeds that much for that long, I figure it needs stitches. Well, how was I supposed to drive myself to the doctor and handle five children with a profusely bleeding thumb? Just at that moment, Mike's offer came to mind. I picked up the phone and dialed his number, quickly explaining my predicament. He rushed right over and helped as best he could. As it turned out, I could not bring myself to ask him to stay with five children or drive me to the doctor for one little old thumb. So I thanked him (again) for helping me and sent him on his way. At that point I realized that I had called him twice and surely must have appeared like the perpetual damsel in distress, and I was supposed to be able to handle living in this new place on my own while managing the children. I then determined that I would not call Mike again, no matter what. I could handle things. If not, I would have to call someone other than Mike.

During that month, my sister-in-law Earla came for a visit. Sometime during that stay, I explained to her how helpful Mike had recently been. As it turned out, Mike and

Earla had grown up near one another in Missouri. I don't think I will ever forget what Earla said to me while we were briefly discussing Mike. She said, "Cheralea, you will not ever find a better man to be a stepparent for those kids than Mike." At the time, I just tucked away that bit of information as "helpful to know" but didn't really dwell on it.

After that, the months sped by as the new school year began. I was more than overwhelmed with my commute, lesson plans, the many, many details of single parenting four kids, and learning to fit into my new world as a single. Sometime in the fall, the drama director of our church approached me about playing the main role in our upcoming Christmas musical. I tentatively agreed; however, I was concerned about who my counterpart would be. The storyline was that of a young couple who were struggling financially. The young lady untimely finds out she is pregnant, and her scared husband is not too happy about it. I really liked the plot line, but as a new single, I was very concerned about who my husband would be on the stage.

For several weeks after agreeing to take on the role, I asked about my counterpart. Finally, Don, the director, said, "I think I have persuaded him to agree. He has been quite busy with a second job, but he did such a good job in the Christmas musical a few years ago, I think he will do it. You know Mike Purcell, don't you?" On the one hand, I was relieved that I would not be "married" to an already married man. On the other hand, I was not happy to be paired with an available single. What would people think? Those fears only lasted about a week. At our second practice for the musical, we rehearsed the scene when "my husband" was supposed to come in the door and briefly kiss me hello. As with all previous close-contact parts I had played, my counterpart and I always played it safe and kept the real thing to a minimum and sometimes didn't actually kiss or twirl or hug until the final dress rehearsal. However, this time was totally different. During that early practice when Mike was supposed to kiss me, he did just that! I was so taken aback I think I was in shock. In fact, Don said, "Wow! That seemed so natural! Shall we do it again?"

Mike was completely red in the face from embarrassment, and I was in heaven. Was this the beginning of something? A couple of weeks later, I finally worked up the nerve to call Mike to ask for a copy of his script, as I had misplaced mine. I carefully chose my outfit. I prayed all the way to his house. I was going to be bold enough to ask him out to dinner. When I rang the doorbell, however, I was terribly disappointed to find another woman in his living room, crawling over piles and piles of school stuff. Thankfully, she was his married next-door neighbor, who was the librarian at their school. However, just her presence there was enough to scare me off from asking him out on the date. I picked up the script and thanked him (again) and drove on home, but not before putting his phone number in my cell phone!

During the course of our relationship at rehearsals, I discovered that along with being a schoolteacher, Mike was also putting in some hours at the local movie rental place in order to pay for some classes he was taking. *Hmmm*, I thought, *movie rentals? I like movies. Perhaps I should frequent the movie rental store when he is working.*

*Why not take this thing for a ride and see where it goes?* I got the feeling Mike was not the ask-a-girl-out type of guy. But I also knew from another friend that he was not adverse to marriage and family; he just had not found the right person. In fact, he had all but given up on ever marrying and having a family. He had simply gotten to the point of praying that if God had a special someone for him, God would have to deliver her right to Mike's doorstep. (You know, sometimes God answers our prayers more specifically than we even intended!)

The fall continued to grow colder, but I felt our relationship warming up. I saw Mike at least once a week at our rehearsals and sometimes more often if I caught him at the movie store. Just before Thanksgiving, I was scheduled to travel to Nashville for an English teachers' conference. I was looking forward to the trip but really dreading the upcoming holidays. As it turned out, I was not going to have the children with me for much of Thanksgiving, so I was looking forward to eating cold turkey from the deli all by myself. Just before I left town, I sent Mike an e-mail asking him to remind Don that I would be missing our next rehearsal. I got on a plane with a couple of my friends and flew to Music City for the conference.

A friend from years back lived in the Nashville area, so we had planned that on one of my free evenings she would pick me up at my hotel and drive me to her friend's home where there was to be a small singles party consisting of her Christian singles group. Talk about out of my element! I only knew one person there, I was out in the middle of nowhere with no transportation of my own to leave the unfamiliar situation, and they were even danc-ing! I am a terrible dancer! The thought occurred to me that I might be able to check my e-mail from the hom-eowner's computer, so with boldness, I asked my friend if that was possible. Shortly afterward, I was hooked up to the Internet in a back bedroom, where I could escape the madness of single life in the living room. When I logged on to my e-mail account, Mike had answered my e-mail! His response simple said, "I'll let Don know. By the way, if you don't have any plans for Thanksgiving, you are wel-come to join the Purcells."

Now there was dancing in the back bedroom too! I'm sure my feet were not on the floor. I had a date, of sorts! At least I was not going to have Thanksgiving dinner alone. But who were the Purcells? Was I eating this big meal with his entire extended family? Yikes! That would be scary. But I couldn't just show up over at his house without spending some time with him first. So I cooked up another plan.

I asked Mike if he would be willing to come over to my house on the day before Thanksgiving to help me move my Christmas decorations into the house from the garage. Of course, he agreed to help and showed up promptly on time. Now I knew this wasn't just a time to move boxes. Even the other lady teachers at his school knew that. They all kept telling him it was a date. "No," he said. "I am just going over there to help her move boxes." (Some men just don't catch the hints, do they?) Move boxes, he sure did! Before he was done with that, he had organized my entire garage, taken down all the fall decorations, and helped put up the Christmas ones.

At one point I asked if he had ever seen the movie *Facing the Giants*. I had heard good things about it and wanted to see it. This time he caught the hint! A few minutes later he asked if I would like to go see the movie with him that afternoon! Yeah for me! I showed him my computer so that he could look up the information on the show times. Unfortunately, the movie had just gone out of the theaters, but he couldn't exactly un-invite me, could he? So we looked for another movie to watch. In the end, we spent over seven hours together that day, just working, playing, and getting to know each other.

The next day, Thanksgiving Day, my parents decided to come to town for dinner, and the meal was wonderfully shared with Mike and his parents, and me and my parents. So you know that old fear of meeting the parents? Well, we each met the other's parents on our second date! Awkward? Kind of. Mike was scared to death. I could tell he was just short of a nervous breakdown. But our parents did a great job of refraining from embarrassing either of us during that occasion, and the meal was fabulous.

My parents and I were going to leave town just after the meal to head to Oklahoma City to spend the rest of the holiday weekend with my brother. But how could I just leave town after that meal with Mike and his parents? Well, I needed to at least extend another word of thanks, so I shot off an e-mail just before we headed south. Of course, my brother had Internet too, so I checked for a response from Mike as soon as we arrived at my brother's house. And yippee! Mike had responded. In fact, he had complimented me in several ways and opened the door for further conversations to get to know each other. I lost count of how many e-mails flew back and forth during those two days, but the relationship was blooming and neither one of us could have been happier. We both felt like giddy high-schoolers experiencing this type of romance for the first time.

At this point, I had been single for eight months. In my estimation, that fell way short of the advised two and one-fourth years. But hadn't I prayed for God to heal me, work in me and through me, and bring me the person he wanted me to have if that was his will? Hadn't Mike been praying fervently for years for a spouse with whom to share the rest of his life? Some people who watched our relationship were afraid we were rushing things. Many thought they were doing the right thing by giving us their words of caution and wisdom. And do you know what? They probably were right in some ways. It is always our duty as Christian brothers and sisters to help each other along on this journey of life. Words of wisdom and caution are part of that help. However, no matter how things appear to those on the outside of the relationship, God cannot be put into an equation. His timing does not always line up with the words of caution from our dearest of friends.

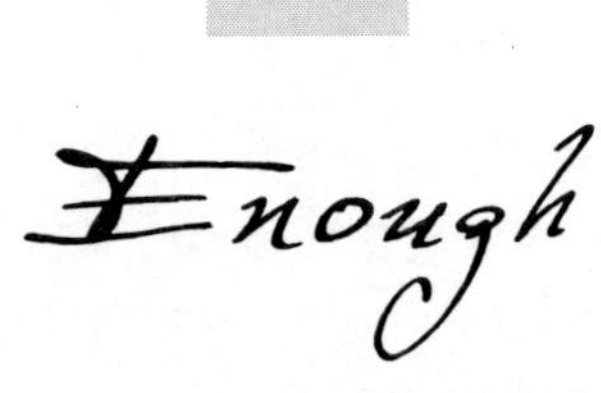

# Enough

## More Than One's Share of Hardship

The day after the highly successful Christmas production, I headed into surgery to have a diseased thyroid removed. For the better part of a year, I had been having all sorts of problems from shakiness to weakness to loss of hair. After a routine checkup, it was determined I was having thyroid problems. So Mike drove me to the hospital in the wee hours of the morning to undergo a rather routine surgery. It all went well, and I was headed home to recover after just a couple of days.

At my one-week checkup, however, I received shocking news. My doctor entered the room and simply said, "I have no idea why you chose to have your thyroid removed, but I am really glad you did. The pathology reports show that both sides of it were cancerous." Okay. Wait! Did I hear him right? I had cancer? People die agonizingly cruel deaths from all different kinds of cancer! I left that doctor's office after I was scheduled to see another specialist and plan out further treatment. I called my mom while walking through the corridor of the hospital. "Mom," I said, "it's not over. I have cancer."

It was a very short drive to the nearby mall where Mike had taken the kids to let them play. He met me in the parking lot and strapped in the kids snuggly. When he turned around, I said those three words again. "I have cancer." I wondered if my life would ever be the same. I couldn't pursue my wonderful, miraculous relationship with Mike without dealing too with this cancer. So later that week, we sat down to discuss the future—our future together and the future with cancer in the picture.

Mike and I had already been talking about getting married and thought that perhaps a summer wedding would be perfect. We could each teach for another semester and take our time in planning the wedding. However, we were so head-over-heels in love that we simply did not want to wait that long. Mike had waited thirty-eight years. Every night when he left and drove home in the snow, I ached from head to toe. I wanted to be a complete family with Mike leading our home. So we then considered a spring break wedding. That would be in the middle of March. This schedule would give us about three months to plan, organize, and finalize the multitude of details in owning one home (Mike's) and renting another (mine). However, after consultation with my doctors, I had to begin weaning off of my thyroid replacement medication and undergo radiation within one month. While it appeared that all the cancer was gone after the surgery, we could not be certain.

After a teary and emotional conversation, Mike and I approached his parents with our problem. Mike wanted to be an active participant in the medical process of helping me deal with the cancer. He didn't want to have to go home every night and leave me in the care of others. He wanted to care for me and for the children. He needed to express his love through his servant's heart. However, to do so would mean to bump up the wedding by several weeks. The best solution we could figure out was a wedding in early February, just five weeks or so away. I fretted over what our parents would say. I worried over how our friends would react. And I simply did not even want to think what my high school students at school were going to say and do!

However, when we talked with Mike's folks, his mom's reply was astounding. In all seriousness, she responded, "Well, why don't you just go down to the courthouse tomorrow?" Okay, now even I think that is rushing it! It was so nice to be supported and loved by our families from the very beginning of our relationship, clear through the hurts and beyond. Neither set of parents felt we should wait. Neither set bought into the marital equation of waiting many months before dating or remarriage. All four of our parents are strong evangelical Christians who believe in the power of prayer and in God's healing and restoring power. They knew that Mike and I were not in high school. We were not approaching our relationship with rose-colored glasses. We knew where we had been, what we had together, and where we wanted to go in the future. We were also committed to the institution of marriage and the commitment for a lifetime. Our godly parents trusted us in all these matters.

I wish I could say that everyone felt the same way about our decision, but they did not. A good friend at church pulled me aside one day and asked, "You are not settling, are you?" In my heart, I cried out, *Settling for what? The first man I have met in twenty years who knows how to treat a lady like a princess? The only man I know who literally lays down his money, his time, and his life for me and the children? The person I want to be with more than any other on the planet? No, I am not settling. I am getting exactly what I have longed for my entire life.* Praise be to God! Some things simply cannot be explained to others who feel so strongly that they are doing us a favor with their words. This analogy just kept coming back to me over and over again during this time:

Life is like a big football game. There are a certain number of players on the field at any given time. Those on the field are the ones in the real battle of life. Their battle can be one of heartache, grief, illness, loss, financial stress, etc. These folks need to be cheered on by all the other people in the stands. However, many times, the fans stand on the sidelines of the game and boo and hiss at the plays of those who are in the game. No one in the stands at any game of any kind, be it football, baseball, or hockey, can truly make a judgment call on what should be done without actually being in the game himself. Those in the stands make judgment calls based on the limited information they can see from their vantage point. They do not see or understand the myriad of details that complicate each decision. One person yelling on the sidelines does not always make the right calls for your life. That is why you need to be constantly in the Word of God, searching for answers directly from him. His ways are always best. His ways are even better than the ways of those who give you wise counsel.

One night my dear friend June met me for dinner at my favorite restaurant to catch up on the details of my confusing life. Frankly, I was nervous about telling her that Mike and I were going to get married in about a month. I needed her to be supportive of me. I wanted her to trust me with such major decisions. As it turned out, she was so impressed with my decisions, discernment, and walk with God that she couldn't help but trust me in this major matter as well. When she shared these things with me, I broke down crying. I was so relieved to know that she was not going to stand on the sidelines and yell at me. She was not going to spend our evening trying to talk me out of marrying Mike or moving up the wedding. She became a cheerleader for us. She was a real friend. She listened to me, expressed her support, and left the rest with the Lord.

When word got out that we were going to be married exactly one month from our engagement day (New Year's Eve), some people were surprised, but on the whole, most people quickly moved beyond that and threw their efforts and energies into helping us have a wonderful wedding ceremony, just in time to beat the throes of radiation. In thinking about what kind of wedding I wanted, I was continually faced with fatigue. I was already emotionally spent from single parenting, running my own home, finding myself in love again, and dealing with cancer. The concept of planning a wedding and seeing it all through to fruition was far too daunting for me. Besides, in my heart of hearts, I didn't think I deserved another nice, big wedding. My first wedding had been the one of my dreams. I simply didn't think I should get the chance to do it all over again.

But what about Mike? He had waited so long for the opportunity to have a beautiful wedding. He had spent lonely nights dreaming about the ceremony, his bride walking down the aisle, witnessed by all his family and friends. Well, that left me with two choices. Either pick the easy way for my tired, old bones or help give Mike the ceremony of his dreams. Was there really a choice? Thankfully, Mike's twin sisters took on the lion's share of the planning and execution of the duties. One made all the decorations and put them up. The other made the wedding cake, and her husband built a beautiful prayer bench for us to use in the ceremony. All of our church friends helped by providing various kinds of cakes for our dessert bar. Neither one of us could have asked for a more gorgeous and special ceremony. And when I walked down the aisle for the second time in my life, supported by my parents on either side of me, I knew I was fulfilling one of Mike's dreams.

I will not dwell long on my cancer treatment. Suffice it to say, it was not pleasant. However, I do not know how I would have made it through without Mike's love and support for both the children and me. He stepped in to care for them when I was not able to even be around them. He handled a birthday party and ran the house while I was quarantined by the side effects of radiation. He was nothing short of amazing! And while I will be an active cancer patient for a few more years, we believe that all the cancer has been removed and that the further treatments are just precautionary.

# Starting Over

## Making a Blended Family Work

With the cancer treatments behind me, I was then able to focus on my new family, with Mike as the head of our household. I am no expert on the subject of blended families, but I do think my story can help a few others on this journey. My blended family only involves one set of children. From those that I interviewed and some of my divorced friends, it is clear that when two or more sets of children are involved, things can grow very tense.—*Yours, Mine, and Ours* is a family-friendly movie about two adults who try to make their relationship work in the midst of joining eighteen children together. The sheer number of people and each of his or her feelings and needs can be entirely overwhelming! So for starters, I will just share about my experiences with blending one set of children with their new stepdad, Mike.

From the beginning, Mike and I decided that my four children were the only kids that we were going to have, so we wanted them to be *ours* not just *mine*. This had to be a literal interpretation, so we went about referring to them in this manner. When asked about the children, Mike would say, "*We* have four children—ages ten, eight, six, and three." I would refer to them as *our kids* and so on. Of course, there were times when we would slip up, but we routinely tried to verbalize them as *ours*.

Saying the children were *ours* and owning them as *ours* are two different things, however. For example, whenever decisions had to be made, I tried hard to consult Mike with the problem and have him weigh in on a solution. That way we appeared to be a unified front for the children. We determined right off that we were not going to let the children turn us against each other. They were not going to come between us. So if Mike said no in response to one of the girls, I was sure to follow with the same answer, and vice versa.

Even before our vows were spoken, the children knew where they stood in relationship to Mike. He was their new stepdad. They already had a dad who was regularly in their lives, but this new stepdad would be with their mom all the time. He was not going to leave, sit off in the corner all by himself, or expect their mom to do all chores, decision-making, etc. Rather, Mike and I made very clear the roles and expectations we had for the children and each other. For example, I have never left my children in the care of a person I did not fully trust with their well-being. When they were with their grandparents, Sunday school teachers, teachers at school, bus drivers, and so on, I knew each person's policy for disciplining the children if necessary. The same was now true for Mike. We had private conversations about the best ways to handle each child, but the message given the children was something like this: Kaitlyn, I know you don't agree with Mike's decision, but he is an active parent in your life, he pays for your schooling and ability to do all the fun things you do, and therefore, you will obey him.

I have to be ready to back up Mike at any moment, should the need arise. Truthfully, most of the time, the children understand that he is a parent and has an equal say in the parenting process. To take this a step further, it would be correct to say that I have worked hard to establish Mike as the actual head of our household in the eyes and minds of the children. Many times I am the one orchestrating details with my ex-husband regarding the children, but they also know that none of that happens without Mike's approval. This is a good time for a bit of caution. I can do these things for Mike and the children because I married a giving man. I married one who loves me and the children and only has our best interests in mind. He is incredibly selfless and has a true servant's heart. Unfortunately, not all men who marry into a family have such true motives. There are many who want a ready-made family with someone else (your ex-husband) paying a lot of the bills. Tragically, there are those who have deviant minds and want to take physical, emotional, or even sexual advantage of you or your children. Then there are also those men who are simply on a power hunt and are looking purely for self-gratification. If you cannot trust your man with the highly responsible duties of head of your household, then you should not be with that man. However, if you have found a gem like I have, then you need to build him up! Esteem him! Be openly support-ive and proud of what he does for a living to bring home money to provide for you and the children. Make an effort every day to do things that will tell him that he is special to you and you love and appreciate all he does.

With Mike as a valuable stepdad in the lives of the chil-dren, one of the first issues we faced was that of titles. Of course, I was *Mom*, but what were they supposed to call Mike? A few years back when he was their Sunday school teacher, he was *Mr. Mike*. But going from teacher to stepdad is a big leap. However, a couple of the kids were adamant that they already had one dad and Mike was not taking his place, so the children felt he should not have the same title. Of course, I would love for the children to call Mike by the endearing term of *Dad*. But they did not ask to have two dads. So as long as they understand that Mike is an equal parent in our household, Mike and I do not mind that they call him by his first name. Once in a while, they will slip up and call him Dad, which makes us smile. When David, our youngest, was just three, he used to call him Daddy Mike. And that was the cutest name of all!

Do you remember when you were first married? There

were so many little things that you and your spouse did not do in the same way. For example, which direction does the toilet paper hang from the roll, from the top and over or from the bottom and under? Is the toothpaste tube shared or did you each need one of your own? When blending a family, you must consider all of these types of nuances and multiply it by however many people are getting used to each other. Let's take, for example, the making of cheesy broccoli. I have been raised on making and eating cheesy broccoli. How hard can it be? You boil the broccoli until it is done, drain off the water and then put a few pieces of cheese or a handful of shredded cheese on the broccoli, cover it with the lid, and let the cheese melt. Isn't that how the entire world makes cheesy broccoli? Apparently not!

One Sunday I had dinner almost done but needed to run upstairs for something and asked Mike to drain the broccoli and put the cheese on it. Simple enough. I ran upstairs. When I returned to my beloved broccoli, I was horrified. (Yes, I overreacted.) My cheesy broccoli resembled broccoli soup!

I spun around and said to my darling husband, who was trying to be helpful, "What did you do to my broccoli?"

He said, "I added cheese and milk."

Milk? Who puts milk in cheesy broccoli? (Probably a lot of you!) But I don't!

Another time I nearly died of heart failure was the first time I served dinner for Mike's parents. All the dishes were ready to put on the table, and I asked Mike to put the rolls in a bowl. To my horror, when I turned around,

I saw that Mike had used a colander lined with a paper towel in which to serve the rolls!

Now let's step back a minute and think clearly about colanders and cheesy broccoli. Is either one of these issues truly important? Of course not. Can they grow into a tremendous problem? Absolutely. When blending two people (or six people, in our case), each person comes from an entirely different set of traditions, expectations, and desires. None of us is very proficient at mind reading, so it is best not to try.

After the colander incident, I began asking Mike to talk more to me about why he did the things he did. Case in point: When Mike lovingly offered to put the clean sheets back on all the beds, I noticed that he put the top sheet of each bed on upside down. The underside was facing up. Why would he do that? Didn't he know the top from the bottom? So when I asked him why he did that, he said that he was raised to make beds that way so that the softer side (top) was brushing up against the skin of the person sleeping in the bed, and then when the covers are folded back, the top side that was then the underside would be facing the top again.

There are a few other priceless items that came up during our first few days and months together that really warrant a moment. Ladies, you already know how different men are from us, right? The buttons on their shirts and zippers on their pants are backward. They are visually stimulated, whereas we are emotionally driven. But on top of all of that, each man is different from all the others. So when getting married the second time, do not be too surprised at how different your new mate is from your first one. For example, since there are four children in our home, we have to do a lot of laundry. I don't mind doing laundry; dusting, however, I do not like to do. Yet it never once occurred to me that laundry would not be one of Mike's favorite chores. Looking at it from his perspective, laundry is a frustrating chore. I have grown up with these children since they left my womb. I know one daughter's pairs of socks from the other two. I know who wears the red and white turtleneck sweater. I even usually know when one daughter has passed down an item to the next youngest daughter. But Mike has no idea who wears the Dora the Explorer underwear, and frankly, that is not something he really wants to know.

I cannot ascribe all of the oddities to Mike, however. One night we were lying in bed talking about anything and everything, when the topic of shoes entered the picture. Mike asked something in regard to my *fetish* with shoes. Fetish? I don't have a fetish with shoes! I just own several pairs for each season. And let me be specific here. I do not own two hundred pairs of shoes like some of my high school students! I probably own thirty pairs in all, for all seasons combined. However, to a guy, that is at least twenty-five pairs more than he owns. As we discussed this hot topic further, we decided to count how many pairs of black shoes I own. When the total got to seven or eight, he simply said, "I own one pair of black shoes, so why do you or any woman need more than one pair of black shoes?" How was I supposed to explain that some are flip-flops, some are sandals. Some are high-heeled, while others are swing-backed. A woman simply cannot wear just any pair of black shoes with just any outfit! Wouldn't that be similar to telling a man that he only needs one tie and it will go with all of his suits, sport jackets, and casual outfits? Some things just will not make sense to the other gender. I can say, however, that for the most part, Mike gives me latitude to be me—a female who runs on emotion, likes to talk, and owns several pairs of black shoes.

Another area we faced early on was that of entertainment. A long way back in my life, I determined that I had far better things to do than spend my time in front of a television. In fact, the absolute only reason I even owned a television while I was single was so that I could check on severe weather if the need should arise. Of course, my children like to watch some TV and movies, but I can do without. Mike, on the other hand, is a movie buff. He knows the names of most actors and actresses and which movies and television programs they have starred in. When he was single and exhausted from putting in a long, full day of dealing with first graders, he would go home and flop on his couch with his dog and grab the remote. Many days, he would fall asleep watching a movie or show before dinner. He was not wrong in watching television or movies, and I was not wrong in choosing not to watch them. But when you put these two behaviors together, it leaves only one solution: compromise. Mike no longer comes home from work and flops on the couch. He either helps one of the girls with homework, or he starts supper.

Many nights we watch a movie together in our bedroom after the children have gone to bed, or we go out for our date night and catch a new movie in the theater. We have reached a good compromise in this area of television and movies. We both do those things that are priority before we zone out in front of the television.

Money issues can be a huge problem for any new couple. For this reason, during our premarital counseling sessions, our pastor had us play a little game. He had Mike and me sit in chairs with our backs to each other and gave us each a piece of paper and a pen. He then asked us questions, to which we were to write our responses, without knowing what the other one was writing. One such question was, "How much money do you feel is reasonable to spend on a pair of tennis shoes for yourself?" Another question was, "How much money do you believe you should be able to spend as petty cash without having to discuss the matter with your spouse?" At the time, I did not realize the significance of this little game. As it turned out, Mike and I both wrote that we thought twenty dollars spent on a pair of shoes was appropriate, and we each wrote that twenty dollars of extra spending was the limit without consulting each other. Most couples do not usually write down so many similar answers. However, this exercise helps men and women realize how different perspectives about money can become huge issues in a family. I strongly believe that both people in the marriage partnership should be involved in the process of keeping track of the finances. In my younger years, I was so overwhelmed with the children and home that I really didn't want to be concerned with the finances. However, that only fueled the flames of my ignorance and misunderstanding of what our financial needs really were. No matter who pays the bills, it is important that both people in the relationship are aware of the bills to be covered, the amount of money available, and the need to save.

Do we dare make the leap of talking about the differences in two extended families? Mike's parents have devoted their lives to ministry, just as my parents have. On the whole, we seem to have been raised quite similarly. However, our family time and holiday celebrations were very diverse. First, as an adult, I have never had the privilege of living near any of my immediate family. Mike, on the other hand, has lived near many of his family for most of his adult years. Currently, we live near his twin sisters and their families and Mike's parents. There are lots of nice things about living near family. They can and often want to babysit. They cook wonderful meals. They are constantly available with support whenever needed. However, since I have never had this commodity, it has been overwhelming at times. You see, Mike's sweet mother has the gift of giving. I do not mean she likes to give gifts; I mean she spends all of her free time and spending money on selecting the perfect gifts for each grandchild in the family.

In addition, she loves to entertain a houseful of her family whenever possible. So the Purcell tradition is that whenever a family member has a birthday, we all gather for a big dinner. Did I mention that, in addition to Mom and Dad Purcell, there are nine grandchildren, three children, their three spouses, two nephews and their spouses, and a host of other friends that get a special birthday dinner? And how about Valentine's Day, Easter, Halloween, and any other day that constitutes a good day for us to be together! I could easily be overwhelmed and smothered by all this fantastic family. However, since I can see that I am somewhat out of my comfort zone, I take that into account and try to plan accordingly. And you know what? The longer I am a part of this wonderful clan, the more comfortable I am around all of them. I feel more and more a part of the madness and not just someone on the outside looking in.

They have completely embraced me and made me one of them. Sometimes that gets tiresome, but it is always worth it. I would not trade my new family for anything. My children now have another set of grandparents to call them on their birthdays, pray with them before their first day of school, go shopping with their interests in mind, come to their Bible quizzes, watch them play basketball, and make their favorite meals. They have more cousins to play with, uncles to tickle them, and aunts to read books to them. Can our children ever have too many people showering them with love and affection? I don't think so. They need to feel loved and accepted by as many people on this planet as possible. And there are no better people to start with than one's own extended family, and a blended one at that.

# It's Not Always Easy

## The Hardships and Happiness
## of Blended Families

It is not always easy to blend a family, and one thing that makes it much harder is the on-going presence of your former spouse. In reflecting on my own situation, I openly confess that there have been times when I have wanted my former husband to move to the farthest end of the planet! I have wanted him out of my life and away from the children. But every time my mind wanders to that place, I see the faces of my children and how utterly crushed they would be if their biological dad were to desert them. No matter how hurt and upset I am on certain days, I don't want that for my kids. I want them to feel loved and supported by both of their biological parents and their step-dad and maybe even some day a stepmom. The divorce was never about the children, and I never want them to feel that they are responsible for it. I do want them to continue in a good relationship with their dad, but many times that puts me in a horrible position. So let's discuss what blended families look like when the former spouse is still on the scene.

For starters, let me lay out some ground rules. I hate to have to address these things, but I do want to be perfectly clear. Once you are no longer married to your former spouse, you should no longer be living under the same roof with him or her. Your finances should no longer be joined, and you should share no bank accounts. You are no longer married. You are separate in the eyes of the law and of God. So do not continue on together as a functioning unit because this is no longer true! I do realize that for some financial matters, things do not happen quickly. Case in point: my former husband and I owned a minivan that was not paid off. When we got divorced, I kept that minivan, but his name was still on the title. I tried, on two different occasions, to file for sole ownership of the van, but my income alone was not enough for me to assume the sole title of the vehicle. Now legally, according to the separation of possessions, the van was solely mine, so I was the only one responsible for the payments, insurance, etc.

Yet my former husband's name was still on the title. That one issue could not be resolved until I got remarried, and Mike literally bought the van from me. We then turned around and took out a bank loan to pay off the dealership loan on the van, so the van now belongs to Mike, and his name is the only one on the title.

The point here is that once you are no longer married, you need to work (and sometimes very hard) at getting your life back under your own control. Your former spouse should have no access to your telephone, mail, or e-mail. He should have no access to enter your home, either when you are there or when you are not.

Sometimes, however, the issue does not necessarily involve the physical aspects of remaining together so much as it involves the emotional part. For example, while in Tennessee attending a National English Teachers' Convention, I was talking with another lady (I will call her Pam) at a party. She told me that she had been divorced for over ten years and that she and her former husband were still very close. So close, in fact, that he and his new wife, along with Pam and their two boys, traveled together to all of the games and events that their boys participated in. I remember thinking at that time that this concept of one big happy family just didn't seem right. Even years later, I still believe there is something inherently wrong with pretending that Mike and I, the children, and their dad are all one big family. I realize that when two people have been married and have children together, the children are the obvious link between the two adults. This link does not break or go away. In fact, if anything, the link gets stronger and tighter as the children grow and mature. Yes, both parents will probably attend most of the children's events. And rightly, they should. However, I do believe a boundary line must exist with you and your new spouse on one side of that line and your former spouse on the other side.

You see, there is an unspoken emotional bond between you and your former spouse. No legal document, stamped by the court, is going to sever that bond. In many cases, a new spouse will not be able to sever that bond either. In my case, I was married to my first husband for nearly fifteen years. We had four children together, and we shared everything with each other. Therefore, even when betrayal happened, that emotional bond was ripped and torn, but it was not wiped out. To this day, we understand each other well. I can guess what he is thinking about any certain topic, and he can probably do the same with me. I can watch a movie and think to myself, *I know he would like to see this movie.* But just because my mind is completely used to thinking this way, I have to retrain myself. I have to purposely work to change those old habits. I have a different husband now, and my focus needs to be entirely on him and my relationship with him. So when thoughts come to my mind about my former spouse, I just mentally flip the *off* switch and choose to move my thoughts to something else or someone else.

However, I have seen many women make choices that will not enable them to move into that much-needed off-mode. Shortly after Mike and I were married, we began making plans to move into a new home that would be *ours*. We needed a home that we bought together and built together. We needed to choose the colors for walls and the rugs for the floors. We needed to bond in this way of building our home. It would not have been right for me to ask Mike to move in and sleep in the same house, bedroom, and bed that my former spouse and I had shared. How would that make Mike feel? He would constantly think of what had already happened inside those walls and sheets. He would not feel that our home was his. Rather, he would feel that he was interloping on someone else's property and space. You never want your new spouse to feel that he is playing second fiddle to your former spouse. So do not put your new spouse in that difficult position.

I know that buying and selling property is not an easy thing to do. It is not a decision that can be made and accomplished in a short period of time. However, make every effort you can to set up a home that builds a relationship with your new spouse. And while we are on the subject of homes, do not set up your new home in close proximity to where your former spouse is living. Again, it is not healthy for you to emotionally abuse yourself or your spouse. I live about a fifteen-minute drive from my former spouse. Mike and I feel that this is a good distance. We have drawn clear boundaries in regard to the locations of our homes. I do not think living close to my former spouse's home would have been a good idea. That could have led to children drifting from one house to the other on a regular basis. And I do not believe that is healthy. The courts set up parental visitation times for a reason. The children are with me for certain times and with my former spouse for other times. I do not want the young children aimlessly drifting back and forth between their parents whenever they please.

There are defining moments that teach us lessons. One of the lessons I gleaned was to be prepared in advance for those times when my former spouse will be in attendance at a child's function. Now I rarely go to events without specifically pointing out to the children where I am sitting and where their dad is sitting. Beforehand, we discuss whom they are to sit with, ride with, and be with. That is not to say that if they are to be with me that they cannot go say hi to their dad, and vice versa. Usually after such an event, we all gather around the child to congratulate him or her and then head off in our different directions.

Even with great preparation, there will come times that are not comfortable. In fact, they are downright difficult. One such occasion occurred on our oldest daughter's birthday. It was customary in her class that on the day of a child's birthday, the parents visited the classroom. Kaitlyn, I was told, was to sit on a stool in the front of the room and answer any questions her peers wanted to ask her. The parents were supposed to sit in the back of the room and tell the class a few things about their birthday child that the class would not ordinarily know. Although this situation seems entirely harmless, in my mind, it was a beast. How was I supposed to sit in the back of the classroom with Kaitlyn's dad and pretend that we were happily married?

Up until that time, I had made a conscious effort not to be alone with my former spouse unless Mike was also there. I realized that this scenario did not exactly constitute being alone since there was also a whole room full of fifth graders and a teacher there, but still, I was to be paired off with my former spouse, and that would be entirely too uncomfortable for me. So when Kaitlyn told me what was to happen, I told her that if her dad was going to be there, I would just let him handle it and I would not go. I immediately saw her face fall in disappointment. Every other child in the class had both parents attend. At that moment, my heart fell too. I pled with her to understand how uncomfortable I would be, and she graciously acknowledged that it would be hard and let me off the hook.

However, that night I decided to pray about it. I prayed for wisdom, and more importantly, I prayed for the ability to swallow the humble pill. I realized that Kaitlyn had a mom and dad and she was proud of both of us. She wanted both of her parents to attend her birthday celebration. She wanted to be normal in that setting. I had to remind myself again that the divorce was never about her or her siblings. And if I wanted her to remain as unaffected as possible, I had to deal with discomfort in times like this, swallow that humble pill, show up, and be a happy mom, if for no other reason than to help Kaitlyn celebrate her birthday with her fifth grade class. That is what I did, and I have absolutely no regrets. Sometimes the humble pill is exactly the medicine needed for the cure.

Another emotional hang-up many women have to face is that of co-parenting great children with the man who devastated their lives. Co-parenting is not the same thing as partnership parenting. In a partnership, the couple works together to weave a delicate balance of boundaries, rewards, discipline, and relationship with the children. In co-parenting, many times that balance is thrown out the window and survival techniques are engaged. However, let me submit to you that co-parenting does not have to be brutal. One of the best things I learned in regard to this subject came from a class presented by the State of Kansas. This class requires attendance by all those who had children and were seeking a divorce. In fact, the divorce would not be granted until this class had been attended by both parties of the divorce. The key word I took away from that meeting was *business*. The partnership parenting is gone, so co-parenting takes its place. Co-parenting runs like a business. You and your former spouse are now business partners. Your business is entirely the wellbeing of your children. Your business transactions are all about the wellness of your children. Granted, these phone discussions and e-mails may be in regard to the children's education, health, schedules, etc., but the transactions are about the business of the children.

When you can approach visitation, child support, scheduling, and the myriad of other things from the viewpoint of kid business, it helps you become detached from the emotional aspects that would otherwise be involved. Yes, your feelings have been smashed. Yes, you are crushed, worn out, and abandoned. None of those things has changed. However, if you keep the business at hand all about the wellbeing of the children and not about you, things will go much smoother. I am happy and relieved to say that at three years out from the finalization of my divorce, I rarely think about all the emotional baggage and hurt anymore. I deal with my former spouse every day. Most days we send e-mails and call on the cell phones. We confirm drop-off times and who will pick up from school. We clear future schedules and secure dates for the kids on our calendars for months in advance. We talk about child support money and which child needs new tennis shoes. My relationship with my former spouse is all about one thing. Well, actually, in our case, four things. They are Kaitlyn, Rachel, Meagan, and David. And that is the healthy way to co-parent. I pray that you can work toward that end in your relationship. If you can truly forgive, you can actually co-parent and be about the business of your children.

Just after my separation, I learned that the children were highly interested in the communication that was taking place between their dad and me. Over time, however, I have come to realize that they do not need to know the details of these lines of communication.

Communication is an important factor in any sector of life. And communication between you and your former spouse is absolutely necessary. As I mentioned, I talk with my ex-husband about most everything that involves the children. While it is not my job to keep him abreast of every school activity and church function, I do make sure that he has all the dates and times for the activities. I do not want to further enable him to slip out of the children's lives, so I make sure he has a copy of the same report cards, calendars, and schedules that I get from the schools. Again, I try to keep most of my communication to e-mails so that they can be quick and reliable without getting emotional.

Another key in communicating with your former spouse must be your willingness to be flexible. Upon occasion I need to work late, so I need someone to pick up the kids from school. Calling the kids' dad is always my first option. He wants to spend time with them, he is their biological parent, and he might be free and willing to pick them up. In the same way, I try to be willing to help out if my ex-husband needs my assistance with something.

In an effort to try to further help my former spouse take ownership and responsibility for the children, I ask him to contact teachers, attend conferences, etc. I am fully aware of all that goes on with the children, but all of this information should not have to be supplied by me. Sometimes he needs to see firsthand what goes on in the classrooms. Sometimes he needs to be the one to make the phone call. Not only are these things important for him, but they are also necessary for the children to understand that he is an active participant in their lives and that he is concerned about all of these things.

For the first year or so after our separation, every time the children had homework or especially large projects, I took the brunt of getting all of that done while the children were at my house. It didn't take very many months to realize that I could not handle all of that while only having the children with me two-thirds of the time. Over the months, we have managed to train the children to pace their schoolwork and projects and work on them further in advance than most of their classmates. They cannot procrastinate until the last night because what if they are at their dad's house on the last night before the photo project is due? Their dad does not have the necessary photos for the project! Again, I refuse to be stressed out because the children are careless in their planning. Thus, we stick to a calendar and keep things rolling far in advance. Also, I try to be sure that my former spouse knows what school events and homework and projects need to be worked on while the children are at his house.

There is just one final thing I would like to express about dealing with my former spouse. Sometimes I am so frustrated I can hardly contain myself. I just want to spout off to Mike, my children, my friends, or anyone who will listen. However, as a Christian, that is not the right response. I need to take my anger to the Lord. I need to lay it down and ask God to work through me and in me. I also make this choice in order to save face for my former spouse. No, I don't always want to do that. No, it doesn't always happen. However, his ill deeds are apparent to everyone around me, and I do not need to say or do anything to point them out. Rather, I need to pray that God will bring him into right relationship with Jesus and that I can be a good example to help in that process.

I must admit that the most frustrating thing in my co-parenting journey with my former spouse is the topic of money. It seems that getting child support money is always an issue. Most months I get the payment late, and that causes great stress for me. Several months ago I was so desperate I called a mutual friend of ours, and he gave me great advice. He said, "Life is too short for this. I know you need the money, but can you find a way to live without it? Then if and when you do get child support, it is just that much better. Living month to month in a state of frustration over whether or not he pays the money is just not worth it. Life is too short for that." Well, what was I supposed to say in response? Of course, I was thinking, *I need the child support money to pay the bills and survive the month!* But that was a given. My friend was right; life is too short. So while I still get nervous and need the money, I am working toward letting go of this as well. I am praying and finding other ways to make that money so that the children and I are not dependent on my former spouse for anything, including his child support check.

Life is short, and in so learning, I have discovered that I cannot fix, control, or change my former spouse. In fact, it is not my responsibility, or aim to do so. I have no more control over him or his decisions than I do over the man in the moon. In order for me to rise above the frustrations and obstacles that come along the way, I have to have realistic expectations. There is a difference between hope and expectation. For example, I hope that my ex-husband will pay child support on time, but I do not expect that he will do so. In learning to think this way, I do not set myself up for future let downs. If I don't expect that the child support will be paid by the first of the month, then when it is paid by the fourteenth, I am not as upset. My expectations were fulfilled. If, on the other hand, the child support payment arrives promptly on the first of the month, I have reason to be happy and hopeful that a new habit will be formed. In the end, I cannot control the actions of my former spouse, but I am responsible for my own expectations and reactions.

# Restored

## New Life through God's Faithfulness

This book began as a testimonial of God's amazing work in my life. Through the chapters and stories, I have told how God has proven faithful time and time again. However, this book would not be complete if those things were all it contained. And so, I want to leave you with one more thought.

Recently, I got a phone call informing me of yet another friend who is facing the fire of rejection. Over the course of the past few months, her husband of seventeen years has begun emotionally connecting with an old girlfriend. Then he moved into a duplex with her, leaving my friend and her sons to figure out how to go on with their lives.

For Mandy and many others like her, this book is a message of hope. We who have been rejected have traveled a similar journey. We have gone from being victims to becoming survivors. We have moved from bitterness to forgiveness to complete release. We are now equipped with a new set of life experiences, and we have seen God's people stand in the gap for us. We have a fresh awareness of God and his continual faithfulness to care for our every need. And if we let them, all of these things can make us better people. We can better sympathize with Mandy and others like her. We can stand beside those who are facing our same pain and gently guide them on the road to recovery.

Recently my Sunday school teacher told us of a man he had encountered. This man's body was severely scarred in many places. Apparently he had suffered a great many physical problems during his life. My teacher was reflecting upon the man's positive attitude, considering all the bad things that had happened to him. Do you have any physical scars? I do. In fact, my children often joke about how many surgeries I have had and how many I will have throughout my lifetime. To date, I have undergone six surgeries. Some have left no visible scars; others have left long, jagged-looking scars.

We who have been rejected have been scarred as well. Instead of a jagged line of healed flesh, there is a scar upon the very heart of our beings. We have been changed for life. There is no way to ever forget the depths of hurt and misery we have faced. Those scars symbolize the pain of living in a fallen world. Sin is all around us. Perhaps we have been scarred by our own actions, or maybe the actions of others. Either way, the scars remind us of where we have come from. Today I am approaching the four-year anniversary of the day my first husband left me. I still feel the pain. I am still aware of the depths of rejection. However, my thoughts do not dwell on those things. Rather, I see the rainbow after the storms. I see how Christ has magnificently restored my health, my heart, and my family.

My pastor once stopped me and asked, "Do you ever wonder where Mike was all those years ago when you married your first husband?" I have thought of that many times. In fact, I have often asked myself if I made the wrong decision back in 1991. Did I marry the wrong person? Was he steeped in sin clear back then? How could I have been so foolish? However, when these thoughts come barreling into my head, the Lord is always faithful to remind me of the story of Esther in the Bible. Haman, a power-hungry man of the court, tricked the king into making a law that would have all the Jewish race killed. As a Jew, Esther knew the risks of approaching her husband, the king, without being summoned, but she also knew that she had to save her family and her entire race of people. And it was for this reason that she boldly went before the king. She said, "If I have found favor with you, O king, and if it pleases your majesty, grant me my life—this is my petition. And spare my people—this is my request. For I and my people have been sold for destruction and slaughter and annihilation" (Esther 7:3–4). When the king discovered Haman's deceit, he ordered his men to hang Haman. God used Esther, her boldness, and her marriage to the king to save all of the Jews. In the same way, God can use your darkest times to bring about the greatest rewards of your life.

In 1991, I made the decision to marry my first husband because I prayed about it and I knew that the Lord was going to bless my marriage. And I have four wonderful children because of that union. I do not believe that I made the wrong choice all those years ago. Furthermore, at that time, Mike was not ready to be married. He was dealing with serious issues in his life and would not have been able to handle marriage. So I have to say with Esther that I have been in this position for "such a time as this" (Esther 4:14). As it states in Scripture, there is a season for everything. There is a time to be born and a time to die, a time to cry and a time to laugh (Ecclesiastes 3). There was a time in 1991 when I chose to marry my college sweetheart. Way back then, God knew that I was making a lifelong commitment. He also knew that he would be with me every step of my journey through this life, including through the storms of divorce.

There will be many things in our lives that don't turn out in the way we expected. There will be decisions made by other people that leave lasting scars on our lives. However, God never leaves us to fend for ourselves. Rather, "We know that in all things God works for the good of those who love him, who have been called according to his purpose" (Romans 8:28).

Jesus Christ has picked up the pieces of my broken heart and life and has woven them back together to create a new life for me. My life will never be the same as it was before March 2006, and I can honestly say that I am glad. As much as the hurt and pain were pure torture to endure, I would do it all over again to grow closer to my Lord, Jesus Christ.

We can share our stories to help others because we have been rescued and reconciled. And there is no one better to teach us these lessons than Job. While the book of Job is not an upbeat and happy sort of book from the Bible, it is one that I reflect on often.

> In the land of Uz there lived a man whose name was Job. This man was blameless and upright; he feared God and shunned evil. He had seven sons and three daughters, and he owned seven thousand sheep, three thousand camels, five hundred yoke of oxen and five hundred donkeys, and had a large number of servants. He was the greatest man among all the people of the East.
>
> Job 1:1–3

In the remaining verses of chapters 1 and 2, God basically allows Satan to do anything short of killing Job, in order to test the man, to see if he would remain blameless and upright or if he would curse God, his creator. During Job's first test, Job received word that all of his oxen and donkeys were carried off by an enemy, fire fell from heaven and burned up his sheep and servants, the camels were carried off in a raid, and a desert wind caused a house to collapse on his sons and daughters, killing them all.

Does this sound familiar to you? One sad blow after another. It got worse! Job's second test brought painful sores to Job from the top of his head to the bottom of his feet. His wife mocked his goodness and encouraged him to curse God and be done with all the evil that he was enduring. Then, if that wasn't enough, Job's three good buddies showed up to talk him into turning against God. This conversation between Job and his friends lasts for thirty-four chapters of the Bible. These friends tried every imaginable angle to convince Job to give up on God.

The tenth chapter begins with Job proclaiming how much he hates his very life and gives full rein to speaking about the bitterness in his soul. Yet, in his frustration, he continues to honor God. In chapter 19, Job explains how he feels crushed by the words of his friends, but he remains faithful to his only real friend. Job sat among the ashes of the fires, scraping his scaly, itching skin with broken pieces of pottery, but never turned his back on his Maker.

I have wondered many times about this moment of decision for Job. I have concluded that Job must have truly known the God of chapter 38. Somewhere deep in his heart, Job really knew the awesome and mighty God. Chapters 38 through 41 are some of the most humbling verses in the Bible. In these chapters, the Creator displays his might and power and shows why he is the king of the universe and to be feared. He thunders from the heavens and tells Job that he must pray and intercede for his friends. Then Job 42:10 says, "When Job prayed for his friends, the Lord restored his fortunes. In fact, the Lord gave him twice as much as before"[1] (NLT). Verse 12 of that same chapter goes on to tell us that the latter part of Job's life was more blessed than the first. He had more sheep, camels, oxen, and donkeys. He had seven strapping sons and three beautiful daughters.

He lived another one hundred and forty years and saw four generations of his family.

But wait! In our rush to get to the end of the book of Job, I don't want us to miss one key concept. Did you see it? After Job obeyed God and remained faithful to the Lord, God restored Job's fortunes. Friend, I know God will do the same for you and me. After all we endure through splitting marriages, single parenting, loneliness, and despair, and we have proven faithful to God, he will restore us to new life. Jesus was there for Job, and he was there for me through my divorce. And because of this, I know he will be there to restore your life as well.

Just eight short months after my divorce, I was remarried. And I have now spent three years with Mike and our wonderful blended family. I have no idea where you are on your journey of healing, but I know that God is greater than all the obstacles and problems that you face today. It may be that God will bring a family member or new friend into your life. Maybe he has a new spouse planned for you. Perhaps you are remarried and trying to make your blended family work. Whatever the case may be, God has the answers. He has lovingly picked me up and dusted me off. He has embraced my pain and set me on the right path. He has nurtured my broken spirit and led me to new joyous life. And I pray that on your journey, you too will hide yourself in him and be restored.

# Endnotes

## Chapter One


1    Lipthrott, D. (1996). *Stages Through Divorce*. Retrieved May 31, 2008, from Stages Through Divorce: http://www.michaelstone.net/divstage.html


## Chapter Two


1    Huizena, D. R. (2008). *Woman's Divorce*. Retrieved May 31, 2008, from Signs of Cheating: http://www.womans-divorce.com/signs-of-cheating.html

## Chapter Three

1    Dobson, D. J. (1996). *Love Must Be Tough.* Sisters: Multnomah Publishers.


## Chapter Four

1    Kubler-Ross, E. (1969). *The Kubler-Ross Grieving Cycle.* Retrieved May 30, 2008, from Changingminds.org: gement/kubler_ross/kubhttp://changingminds.org/disciplines/change_manaler_ross.htm

2    Arterburn, Stephen (2004). *Every Heart Restored.* Colorado Springs: WaterBrook Press.

3    Banks, S. (2002). *Anchors of Hope.* Nashville: Braodman & Holman.


## Chapter Six

1    Winchell, Walter. *Thinkexist.com.* Retrieved June 27, 2009 from Thinkexist.com: http://thinkexist.com/quotation/a_real_friend_is_one_who_walks_in_when_the_rest/15163.html

2    Emerson, Ralph Waldo. Thinkexit.com. Retrieved June 27, 2009 from Thinkexist.com: http://thinkexist.com/quotation/a_real_friend_is_one_who_walks_in_when_the_rest/15163.html

3    Peter, Laurence. *Brainy Quotes*. Retrieved June 27, 2009 from BrainyQuotes.com: http://www.brainyquote.com/quotes/quotes/1 /laurencej105237.html

4    Craik, Dinah Mulock. *Moments Like These*. Retrieved June 27, 2009 from MomentsLikeThese.com: http://donna-howey.typepad.com/moments_like_these/2009/03/eric-carles-the-very-hungry-caterpillar-day-march-20.html

5    Emerson, Ralph Waldo. *Thinkexist.com*. Retrieved June 27, 2009 from Thinkexist.com: http://thinkexist.com/quotation/the_glory_of_friendship_is_not_the_out-stretched/9297.html

6    Dave Matthews Band. *Under the Table and Dreaming* (1994). Produced by RCA. New York, New York.

7    Rice, Helen Steiner. (1979). *Everyone Needs Someone: Poems of Love and Friendship*. Fleming H. Revell Co.


## Chapter Seven

1    Hamilton, D. T. (n.d.). *The Stages of Divorce*. Retrieved May 31, 2008, from Gibson Grace & Merrill: http://www.tommerrill.com/pg15.cfm


## Chapter Nine

1    Hamilton, D. T. (n.d.). *The Stages of Divorce*. Retrieved May 31, 2008, from Gibson Grace & Merrill: http://www.tommerrill.com/pg15.cfm

2   Elias, Marilyn. *Psychologists Now Know What Makes People Happy*. USA Today. October 12, 2002.

3   Arterburn, S. (2005). *Healing is a Choice.* Nashville: Thomas Nelson, Inc.

4   Boom, C. T. (1971). *The Hiding Place.* New York: Bantam Books.

5   Swindoll, Charles. *Attitude by Charles Swindoll.* Retrieved June 27, 2009 from Legendary Notes: http://www.geocities.com/livelifeuwant/legn_notes_Attitude.html

6   Chambers, Oswald. (1992). *My Utmost for His Highest.* Discovery House Publishers.

## Chapter Ten

1   Chambers, Oswald. (1992). *My Utmost for His Highest.* Discovery House Publishers.

## Chapter Eleven

1   Gaither, Gloria and William J. (1971). *Because He Lives.* William J. Gaither.

2   Dobson, D. J. (1996). *Love Must Be Tough.* Sisters: Multnomah Publishers.

## Chapter Twelve

1    Glendenning, A. (2006, February 21). *Marriage After Divorce.* Retrieved June 19, 2008, from Families.com: http://marriage.families.com/blog/marriage-after-divorce

2    Cottrill, J. (2008). *Making Your Second Marriage Work.* Retrieved June 25, 2008, from Love and Marriage: http://love.ivillage.com/lnm/0,,npzf,00.html

3    Cottrill, J. (2008). *Making Your Second Marriage Work.* Retrieved June 25, 2008, from Love and Marriage: http://love.ivillage.com/lnm/0,,npzf,00.html

## Chapter Sixteen

1    Holy Bible, New Living Translation. Carol Stream: Tyndale House Publishing, Inc. 1996.